Israel and the Kingdom:
An Eschatology of Victory

Glenn Shaffer

Two Words, Inc.
2300 Southaven Rd.
Claremore, OK 74019

©1999
Revised ©2014

ISBN: 0-9988556-0-X
ISBN: 978-0-9988556-0-8

About the Front Cover

The front cover picture is a reproduction of a lost oil painting titled, ***The Siege and Destruction of Jerusalem by the Romans Under the Command of Titus, A.D. 70*** by David Roberts. Roberts drew upon the writings of Jewish Historian Flavius Josephus, who was an eyewitness to the siege and destruction. This major event predicted and foretold by Jesus in Matthew, Mark, and Luke sets the stage for Jesus' warning, often called the Olivet Discourse, in Matthew 24.

Dedication

It is only appropriate that I dedicate this book to the congregation where my wife and I have led for nearly four decades. This church has been willing to learn, grow, and receive teaching that has challenged them. As a church, during the 1980s, we walked through some growing times, stepping out to embrace a Partial-Preterist view in place of Dispensationalism, in which most of us were brought up. I have a deep gratefulness to this wonderful group of believers who have grown into a powerful influence, literally reaching around the world with the message of the kingdom.

Table of Contents

Preface

Thoughts and ideas have great implications. One's worldview affects how life is lived and values shared. It communicates to others a great deal about one's view of Christ. Theology produces a worldview. Nothing affects our worldview of the future more than the study of last things. Eschatology is the study of last things. It could be said the view of end times says more of one's *Christology* than their *eschatology*. Eschatology determines a worldview. How one views God's work in the world presently, and through the events of history, determines one's understanding of God's dealing with His church and the nations at the present time and in the future. The material in this book supports a victorious Christ and His Kingdom from the time of the cross until the second coming.

My search in the study of last things began in my teen years in the early 1970s. Growing up in an Evangelical and Pentecostal environment my only views of eschatology came from the popular Dispensational teaching. This part of God's Word seemed so fanciful and elusive to the average church member. It seemed that only world travelers, and sought-after speakers and specialists, had anything to say about this doctrine. Normal pastors or church leaders, relied upon traveling experts with their theories and charts. These experts, who were looked upon as authorities on this subject, often quoted the latest news happenings to prove they were "in the know." Often their interpretations required presuppositions beyond the simple reading of the scriptures. Modern day catastrophes and national events in the Middle East were regularly cited to support scriptural texts.

As a young Bible student, I wanted to know how prophecy teachers could know their theories were right? How could they know that Bible prophecy included jet planes, missiles, and atomic weapons? I heard one popular teacher explain that John in the Book of Revelation, and the prophet Ezekiel, did not know what they were seeing so they described what today is known.[1] Weekly predictions were given as proof of the last days. I remember when a famous teacher predicted we were not going to see the end of 1981. The rapture would take place that year to begin a seven-year tribulation with the second coming by 1988. Then the eighties came and went with the embarrassing book by Whisenhunt, *Eighty-Eight Reasons Christ Will Come in 1988.*

My journey on this subject continued through Bible College. Those days were spent doing paper after paper on the subject of the end times. After cornering all the professors on the subject, little satisfaction came forth from my inquiries. The process included stumbling across George Ladd's book, published in 1956, called *The Blessed Hope.* By the end of that year of college I had moved from being Dispensationalist to a Historic-Premillennialist also known as a Post-tribulationalist. Still dissatisfied with many of the scriptures on the subject, the search continued. Something was missing.

The Lord began to deal with me concerning the Church and the Kingdom during the early 1980s while I was a young pastor.

---

[1] Hal Lindsey, *The Late Great Planet Earth* (Grand Rapids, MI: Zondervan Publishing House, 1980) 150.

Understanding began to come on the scriptures concerning the New Testament function of the church and its government. The purpose of the Church to extend the Kingdom of God, became a central focus. With this emphasis of the purpose of God in the earth, it brought back to the forefront the subject of eschatology. Some key pieces began to fall into place when, providentially, I picked up a newly-released book in 1985 by David Chilton, entitled *Paradise Restored*. While reading the book on the plane coming back from a conference in Georgia, I knew I had discovered some missing links. Many pieces were coming into place and came quickly. I realized I was no longer a Historic-Premillennialist; I could see the purpose of the Kingdom in the earth for today. Much reading and research has followed, but my confidence has grown stronger that the church must return to a more orthodox view of Christ's Kingdom. God has a work to do through the church before Jesus returns.

The purpose of this material is to present the orthodox teaching of the scriptures concerning the second coming of Christ and His present reign. It is to take a look at the study of last things in light of the *Partial-Preterist* view. *Preterist* means completed. We say partial in view of the fact that much of the Olivet discourse in Matthew 24, Mark 13, and Luke 21, are seen as being fulfilled in the first century. The Book of Revelation is primarily a larger view of the same prophecy. We are not presenting a *Full-Preterist* view in light of the fact there still remains the last day resurrection and the literal second coming of Christ. We hold to the orthodox view that Christ will physically and literally return in power and great glory to judge the living and the dead.

My goal is to bring a better understanding on the present reign of Christ and the study of last things among those who will read this material, but maybe not read others. This material is no test of fellowship, or authenticity of one's salvation. Though we teach this subject with great confidence, we have respect for others who see it differently. In our attempt to recover what we see as accurate, may this subject never become the point of division or proof of orthodoxy of one's faith in Christ.

Introduction

Israel and the Kingdom: An Eschatology of Victory, is an interactive book presenting a Partial-Preterist view of the study of last things. The reader will be given a clear overview of where the teaching is headed, and then a fuller explanation of a victorious eschatology.

Eschatology affects a person's worldview and outlook of the future. It can be said your eschatology, or study of last things is determined by your Christology—how you view the work of Christ in the earth today. This study guide will walk you through God's work in parts of history, and His dealing with His church and the nations at the present time and in the future.

Jesus Prophesied the Last Days

This teaching presents Jesus' prophecy in Matthew 24, often referred to as the *Olivet Discourse*, as His exact prediction of the impending judgments upon apostate Israel within that generation. When Jesus declared, "This generation will not pass away until all these things be fulfilled" (Matt 23:36; 24:34), He meant what He said. Those were the *last days* of which Jesus prophesied. With the impending end of the days of Moses and the Old Covenant, Christ would be bringing about a new day called the Messiah's Day. This was the fulfillment of all that the prophets declared. It was to be brought forth through the ascension and reign of Christ as predicted by Daniel the prophet (Daniel 7:14), and explained by Peter the apostle (Acts 2:29-36).

These chapters include a presentation of passages from the Old Testament, New Testament, and recorded history, to show that when Jesus spoke of His coming in power and great glory, He spoke of His resurrection, ascension to the throne of David, and His coming in judgment to Jerusalem. As the result of His reign in heaven, there was a fulfillment of prophecy of which He spoke. This prophecy included a time of great tribulation and judgment upon what the book of Revelation calls the apostate Jerusalem, the great whore. It includes Rome, known as the beast from the sea. The judgment upon those who rejected the Messiah culminated in the time of war and destruction of the temple in 70 AD, just as Jesus prophesied: "Upon you will come all the righteous blood that has been shed on earth" (Matt 23:35).

The destruction of Jerusalem and the temple was a sign to the Jews, Christians, and the world, that God had wrought a mighty transformation from one covenant to another. Although Jesus' work at the cross legally and definitely ended the days of Moses, the Jews of that generation continued to offer sacrifices and offerings until the destruction of Jerusalem. They carried on as if the Son of God, the Messiah of Israel, had not come. Surely, He had come unto His own and His own received him not (John 1:11). They were blinded to the Messiah and carried on with the temple worship even though one greater than the temple had come. Apparently, they sewed the torn veil back together and ignored the coming of the Son of God. This was not only a grievous matter to God, it was a hindrance to the Church of Christ. It was the full rejection of the Messiah and the plan of God through Abraham (Gen. 12:3; Gal. 3:16).

Scripture references to the *last days*, unless connected with the resurrection on *the last day*, refer not to the final coming of Christ in the distant future, but the last days of Moses' government of the Old Covenant. The days of God's people under Moses came to an end as a result of the cross of Christ. For now, one greater than Moses was the builder of the house, and not just a servant of the house (Heb. 3:1-6). When the Bible says, "Jesus has appeared to put away sin at the end of the ages" (Heb. 9:26), it means the end of Moses' age. Paul wrote to Timothy and his contemporaries that perilous times were coming in the last days (2 Tim. 3:1). He was speaking of the last few years before Christ came in judgment against the holy city of Israel that had become a place of desolation. The apostles knew this was a predicted work of God, for they were the words of Jesus, the Son of God. These things were a sign that Jesus was the Messiah, and that He was ruling from the heavens. This was to be the sign that the Son of man was in heaven.

The Church—His Eternal Purpose

God's purpose for His church is to demonstrate the Kingdom of God in the earth through His plan that began in the garden of Eden. His eternal plan is to have a people manifesting His kingdom, and that purpose has continued to this day. It will always be His purpose because it is called the *eternal purpose of God* (Eph. 3:9-11). He chose Abraham through whom to bring forth the *seed*, who is Christ, so all the nations of the earth would be blessed. Christ was the fulfillment of God's promise to Abraham, and those of *faith* have always been, and will always be, the children of Abraham. God is not married to two brides but one: the church. God is not in two covenants, one with natural Israel and one with the Church. He has always had one promise brought forth through two covenants. The first covenant was called Moses' day, and the second, or better covenant, called Christ's day. The fulfillment of the promises and everlasting covenants are made with those of faith and not of race. Natural Israel has fulfilled its purpose and God's dealings with natural Israel are finished. First the natural and then the spiritual. It is not *replacement* theology, but rather *fulfillment* theology. God's eternal plan has always been, and always will be, to have a people in which He may dwell and be as one with His bride. Christ came to fulfill all that the prophets declared. His promises made to Israel forever are fulfilled in His people the Israel of God (Gal 6:15-16).

Views of the Millennium

There are three interpretations of eschatology in relationship to what is called the millennium. Although the word millennium is in not in the Bible, it comes from two Latin words: *mille* meaning thousand, and *annus* meaning years. The reference is taken from Revelation 20.

Premillennialism

The prefix "pre" indicates that Jesus returns before the millennium, or a thousand-year reign. Premillennialism teaches Jesus will return before a literal thousand-year reign. After He returns, He will rule the earth from Jerusalem in Palestine. On the earth will be natural people, those who made it through the tribulation, but missed the rapture of the church and had babies during the millennium. The resurrected and raptured saints, and natural Jews who have become believers during the tribulation period, also live together. Natural people from all over the world will travel to Jerusalem from year to year to offer blood sacrifices as a memorial to God. This reign will last for a literal 1000 years. At the end of this millennium, there will be a new heaven and new earth with the Holy City (heaven) coming down to the earth. The saints will live in the city, but the natural people must stay outside of the city. This will continue throughout all eternity.

Dispensationalism is a form of Premillennialism. Dispensationalism teaches that God deals with man differently in seven different time periods. It teaches that we are presently living in the Church Age as the sixth dispensation, and the kingdom of God is future, called the seventh dispensation. Premillennialists, who believe Christians will go through a seven-year tribulation period are called Historic-Premillennialist or Post-tribulationist. Dispensationalists, however, believe that Christians will not have to go through a seven-year tribulation period. They believe that there will be a secret coming of Christ to snatch people away,[2] leaving the wicked and unbelieving here on the earth to go through a seven-year tribulation after which Jesus will come again. Then He will reign on earth with His throne in Jerusalem for a thousand years. Animals will get along in peace, and corporations will do business in agreement, while the battleships of the earth rust from nonuse.[3] At the end of the millennium He will come again for the final judgment when Satan is cast into the lake of fire.

Amillennialism

The prefix "a" means "no millennium." Amillennialism sees the thousand year reign representing Christ's present reign. This view of eschatology, involves the rejection of the belief that Jesus will have a literal, thousand-year-long, physical reign on the earth. It teaches there is no particular time in history where the gospel has a greater effect in society, but rather, the wicked and the righteous

---

[2] Tim LaHaye, *The Beginning of the End* (Wheaton, Il: Tyndale House Publishers, 1982) 21.
[3] Clarence Larkin, *The Greatest Book on Dispensational Truth in the World* (Philadelphia, PA: Rev. Clarence Larkin Est., 1920) 94-95.

grow together as wheat and tares until the end. This teaching simply sees the thousand-year reign as the time from the first advent to the second coming. It has had a favorable embrace throughout church history and today among many denominations.

Postmillennialism

The prefix "post" means that Christ will come after a long successful time of the Gospel called the millennium. Postmillennialism teaches that Christ will return at the end of history when the nations have been widely affected by the gospel. The millennium is not seen as a literal 1000 years, but as long successful time in history where the gospel is victorious upon the nations. It does not suppose a utopia, nor does it presume everyone is saved, but a definite time in history where there is a change in the order of society by the saving grace of Christ in the lives of individuals. This view holds that Christ will literally return at the end of history to judge the living and the dead. Eternity will begin with the Kingdom being turned over to the Father.

The Apostles' Creed which was first recorded in the fourth century is believed to have been around from the declarations of the early apostles. It more closely reflects the amillennial or postmillennial view and not the premillennial view. Dispensationalism did not exist at the time of the Apostles' Creed. The creed declares, "On the third day he arose again. He ascended into Heaven, and is seated at the right hand of the Father. *He will come again to judge the living and the dead.*" (Emphasis mine.) If the church fathers believed a dispensational view, then the creed would have reflected it.

The Messiah's Day began with His ascension into heaven and the outpouring of the Holy Spirit on the Day of Pentecost. It is referred to as the reign of Christ and will continue until He comes again; then He will turn the kingdom over to the Father. The gospel will have a widespread and successful affect upon the nations of the earth. History will culminate with the literal return of our Lord and Christ, and time will be no more.

Four Principles of Interpretation

Certain principles should be adhered to in order to maintain integrity in interpreting the scriptures. These principles avoid personal application of meaning and presuppositions. It takes discipline to hold to these principles when they fly in the face of our preconceptions.

Comparative Revelation: This order of interpretation allows the scripture to interpret the scripture. Great confidence can be given to this type of interpretation. This is particularly useful when examining apocalyptic and end-of-the-world language. Interpret the Bible in light of the Bible. When we allow the New Testament apostles to tell us the meaning of Old Testament prophets, we have truly discovered the foundation of the church. Though I believe apostles and prophets still exist in the church today, I think the meaning of Ephesians 2:19-22 is most fully understood in the light of the church being built upon the foundation of the New Testament apostles and the Old Testament prophets. That is, the words of the Old Testament prophets are interpreted by the New Testament apostles, ". . . you are . . . of the household of God, having been built on *the foundation of the apostles and prophets*, Jesus Christ Himself being the chief corner stone, in whom the whole building, being joined together, grows into a holy temple in the Lord, in whom you also are being built together for a dwelling place of God in the Spirit." (Emphasis mine.)

Contextual Revelation: Interpret the scriptures in light of the context. This principle is commonly ignored. Too often verses are taken out of context and made to mean something entirely different. This means of interpretation should always be used. There may be allegorical benefits to scriptures, but the context is the authority for interpretation.

Clear Revelation: Interpret the difficult passages in light of the clear passages. This is similar to biblical hermeneutics. We include this principle, however, to keep the meanings interpreted in light of already easily accepted revelation. Do not do the opposite and try to understand the clear passages by the difficult ones.

Comprehensive Revelation: Interpret scriptures within the scope of the whole counsel of God. Scriptures, even in context, still need to be placed within the wider view. This prevents doctrine from being built upon isolated passages. The overall theme of God's purposes and plan gives stability in interpretations. The Bible gives us the master plan of God for the ages.

Introduction
Discussion Questions

1. What does the word millennium mean?

2. Identify the three main interpretations of the 1000-year reign.

3. Dispensationalism comes under which of the three main interpretations?

4. Dispensationalism teaches that God deals with man differently in each dispensation of time. Name the period of time in which we presently live according to dispensationalism.

5. How many resurrections are taught under dispensationalism?

6. List each of the three resurrections in dispensationalism.

7. List the four principles of interpretation.

SECTION I

CHAPTER 1

Who is the Israel of God?

Who is the Israel of God? What does "Israel" mean? Israel was the personal name of Jacob, given to him by God in Gen. 32:28. And He said, "Your name shall no longer be called Jacob, but Israel; for you have struggled with God and with men, and have prevailed."

According to *Smith's Bible Dictionary*, Israel means, "the prince that prevails with God." It has also been interpreted as "God rules," and "God prevails." The name was applied to the Hebrew people in Exodus. "Afterward Moses and Aaron went in and told Pharaoh, Thus says the LORD God of Israel: Let My people go, that they may hold a feast to Me in the wilderness" (Exodus 5:1).

This name was also applied to the remnant of people who remained believers in the one true God. A remnant means the left-overs. To have a remnant meant many had fallen away and only the true believers remained as the remnant. They were still called Israel. Here we see that true Israel were those of faith. The prophet Jeremiah declared, "Thus says the LORD of hosts: They shall thoroughly glean as a vine the remnant of Israel; as a grape-gatherer, put your hand back into the branches" (Jer. 6:9).

The Seed of Abraham

When we come to the New Testament, we discover important passages of the scriptures concerning Israel. In Romans 9 and 11, Paul refers to "physical Israel" and "spiritual Israel." He does so by saying that all who are of the natural descendants are not necessarily Israel. Beginning in Romans 9:1, Paul grieves over the fact that his kinsmen after the flesh, are not turning to Christ as he would desire for them to do. He grieves because he knows that unless they accept the same Christ in the same way as do the Gentiles, they are not "true Israel," and therefore would be accursed. His statement in Romans 9:6 is in defense of the Word of God. He knows the promise of God to Abraham, but he declares their falling away is not a reflection on God's word, but rather all Israelites are not all true Israelites. He writes, "But it is not that the word of God has taken no effect. For they are not all Israel who are of Israel."

What is Paul saying when he declares, "not all who are called Israel are Israel?" He is saying, just because they belong to the natural nation of Israel, that does not make them a part of true Israel. He goes on to say, "Nor are they all children because they are the seed of Abraham" (Rom. 9:7). Belonging to the natural seed of Abraham does not qualify them as the Israel or the chosen of God. That is a big statement in light of the dispensationalist teaching that God has a covenant with Israel that is independent of their faithfulness. Lest we misunderstand what Paul is saying, he declares it even more clearly: "That is, those who are the children of the flesh, these are not the children of God; but the children of the promise are counted as the seed" (Rom. 9:8).

Who then are the children of promise? We are not left to wonder about this either. In Galatians 3:6-9, once again Paul, who was given this mystery, elaborates on the concept that the promise came to Abraham by faith, therefore, it has always been by faith and not by race. Here Paul declares:

Just as Abraham believed God, and it was accounted to him for righteousness. Therefore know that only those who are of faith are sons of Abraham. And the Scripture, foreseeing that God would justify the Gentiles by faith, preached the gospel to Abraham beforehand, saying, "In you all the nations shall be blessed." So then those who are of faith are blessed with believing Abraham.

We know that Christ was the Seed; therefore, all Abraham's seed are those who have their faith in Christ Jesus. Paul tells us only those who believe are sons of Abraham: "Therefore know that only those who are of faith are sons of Abraham" (Gal. 3:7). "Only those who are of faith," is a very important statement because he is speaking of those who have faith in Jesus Christ and none other.

Jesus dealt with this same issue when He made a distinction between Jews who believed in Him and those who did not. Then Jesus said to those Jews who believed Him, "If you abide in My word, you are My disciples . . . They answered Him, We are Abraham's descendants . . . Then Jesus replied, I know that you are Abraham's descendants, but you seek to kill Me, because My word has no place in you . . . You are of your father, the devil . . ." (John 8:31, 33, 37, 44).

John the Baptist spoke almost these same words to the Jewish leaders of his day when he said, "...and do not think to say to yourselves, 'We have Abraham as our father.' For I say to you that God is able to raise up children to Abraham from these stones. And even now, the ax is laid to the root of the trees. Therefore every tree

which does not bear good fruit is cut down and thrown into the fire"
(Matt. 3:9, 10).

Both Jesus and John the Baptist are plainly saying that those
who believe on Jesus are the true "children of Abraham." In spite
of these strong arguments, some still say that natural Israel has a
covenant through Abraham apart from Christ. Their understanding
is that God will give natural Israel of today a second chance as the
nation favored by God. In the future, natural Israel will all come to
know Jesus, born of Mary, as Christ. This belief is based upon the
understanding that God has made a covenant with natural Israel
through Abraham and it was not fulfilled in Christ through the
gospel being preached in history, but will be fulfilled in the future
during a time of a millennium reign.

The Mystery of God

So much of Paul's message was on the subject of all believers being
one in Christ. He spoke concerning the church as the true Israel
made up of all those who are of faith. He tells us that it was the
mystery of God. He expounds on this mystery in this passage.

> *If indeed you have heard of the stewardship of the grace of God,
> which was given to me for you, how that by revelation He made
> known to me the mystery (as I wrote before in a few words, by
> which, when you read, you may understand my knowledge in
> the mystery of Christ), which in the other ages was not made
> known to the sons of men, as it has been revealed by the Spirit
> to His holy apostles and prophets: that the Gentiles should be
> fellow heirs, of the same body, and partakers of His promise in
> Christ through the gospel. (Eph. 3:26)*

Some teach that Paul saw the church as the mystery, and that
it was not the intended plan of God, but that is incorrect. Notice,

clearly, the mystery was that both Jews and Gentiles were together as *one* in Christ's church. That can't be missed. The body of Christ did not exist until the Day of Pentecost, but we could say the church per se, existed in the Old Testament. The Greek word translated to English as church is *ekklessia,* which literally means the "called out ones." It should be noted this term was used for Israel in the time before the coming of Jesus the Messiah. Therefore, they were called the church or the "called out ones" according to Acts 7:38: "This is he who was in the church in the wilderness . . ." This is important because it shows God's heart to have a people. It was His plan from the very beginning. That is why God declared that the seed of the woman, which is Christ, would crush the head of the serpent, which is Satan (Gen. 3:15). Christ and his Church has always been the focus of the Scriptures. God's plan has always been to have a people in which He may dwell and call His bride.

With the coming of Christ, the favor of God is manifest upon all nations, tribes, and tongues. Christ's inheritance is the nations of the world (Ps. 2:8). The idea of a special, called-out people was the identical concept of Israel. In Ephesians, Paul goes on to emphasize the mystery as God's: "...eternal purpose which He accomplished in Christ Jesus our Lord" (Eph. 3:11).

Paul declares:

Wherefore remember, that ye being in time past Gentiles in the flesh, who are called "Uncircumcision" by that which is called the "Circumcision" in the flesh made by hands; that at that time ye were without Christ, being aliens from the commonwealth of Israel, and strangers from the covenants of promise, having no hope, and without God in the world. (Eph. 2:11-12)

Notice, he speaks of those who "once" were Gentiles. Though Gentiles and Jews remain as they are in the natural, Paul makes it clear that now they are no longer considered Gentiles as far as the plan of God is concerned; a Gentile being those estranged from the promises of God. Paul even says the Gentiles who are called uncircumcised by the Jews, really are not the uncircumcised, but rather are the circumcised. They are just called uncircumcised by those who are not "really circumcised." The natural Jews were circumcised "in the flesh by hands"; therefore, Paul did not consider them as truly circumcised. Why is Paul making such a big deal out of this concept? He did not want there to be a misunderstanding about God's people.

Speaking to these who were former Gentiles, Paul declares the wall of separation between them and the natural descendants of Abraham has been torn down. Through Jesus they have been made as one. The new joining together in Christ is called a "new man." The Gentiles are said to be made fellow-citizens with the saints and of the household of God.

> But now in Christ Jesus, you who sometimes were far off are made near by the blood of Christ. For he is our peace, who has made both one, and has broken down the middle wall of partition between us; having abolished in his flesh the enmity, even the law of commandments contained in ordinances; for to make in himself of two one new man, so making peace; And that he might reconcile both unto God in one body by the cross, having slain the enmity thereby: And came and preached peace to you which were afar off, and to them that were near. For through Him we both have access by one Spirit unto the Father. Now, therefore, you are no more strangers and foreigners, but fellow-citizens with the saints, and of the household of God . . . (Eph. 2:11-19)

Early Church Fathers understood the Church to be the fulfillment of all that the prophets had declared. Below are several instances.

Justin Martyr (100-165 A.D) understood this when he wrote:

Jesus Christ ... is the new law, and the new covenant, and the expectation of those who out of every people wait for the good things of God. For the true spiritual Israel, and the descendants of Judah, Jacob, Isaac, and Abraham (who in uncircumcision was approved of and blessed by God on account of his faith, and called the father of many nations), are we who have been led to God through this crucified Christ. God blesses these people and call them Israel and declared them to be his inheritance, therefore, all who have fled through him to the Father constitutes the Blessed Israel.[4]

Irenaeus, Bishop of Lyons (AD 130-200): *Now I have shown a short time ago that the church is the seed of Abraham.*

Hippolytus of Rome (AD 170-236): *For it is not of the Jews He spoke this word of old, nor of the city of Zion, but of the church. For all the prophets have declared Zion to be the bride brought from the nations.*

The reformers also believed those of faith were the seed of Abraham. Martin Luther clearly explains Galatians 6:16:

Paul adds the words "upon the Israel of God." He distinguishes this Israel from the Israel after the flesh, just as in 1 Cor. 10:18 he speaks of those who are the Israel of the flesh, not the Israel of God. Therefore peace is upon Gentiles and Jews, provided that they go by the rule of faith and the Spirit.[5]

Explaining this same verse, John Calvin says:

Upon the Israel of God. This is an indirect ridicule of the vain boasting of the false apostles, who vaunted of being the descen-

---

[4] Circa AD 160. English translation from the *Dialogue* with Trypho xi, in *The Ante-Nicene Fathers of the Christian Church*, eds. Alexander Roberts and James Donaldson, vol. 1 (Eerdmans, repr. 1987), 200.

[5] English translation from *Lectures on Galatians*, 1519, in volume 27 of *Luther's Works*, ed. Jaroslav Pelikan (Saint Louis: Concordia, 1964), 406.

dants of Abraham according to the flesh. There are two classes who bear this name, a pretended Israel, which appears to be so in the sight of men, and the Israel of God. Circumcision was a disguise before men, but regeneration is a truth before God. In a word, he gives the appellation of the Israel of God to those whom he formerly denominated the children of Abraham by faith (Galatians 3:29), and thus includes all believers, whether Jews or Gentiles, who were united into one church.[6]

A quick look through the Scriptures reveal the Bible holds this to be true that the Old Testament Israel is fulfilled in the saints of the New Testament made up of both Jews and Gentiles.

Old Testament		New Testament
Psalm 89:7	*Saints* or *Holy Ones*	1 Corinthians 14:33
Isaiah 45:4	*Elect or Chosen*	1 Peter 1:2; Colossians 3:12
Deuteronomy 33:12	*Beloved*	Colossians 3:12, Romans 1:7
Isaiah 43:7	*The called*	Romans 1:6; 8:28
Isaiah 40:11	*Flock*	Acts 20:28; Luke 12:32
Exodus 19:6	*Holy Nation*	1 Peter 2:9
Isaiah 62:5	*Bride*	John 3:29

Synagogue of Satan or a Kingdom and Priest

When addressing the seven churches of Asia, the resurrected Christ spoke to the Church in Smyrna and Philadelphia about what He called the synagogue of Satan. He is speaking about those who claimed to be the people of God by calling themselves Jews when they were not. He said, "I will make those who are of the synagogue

[6] John Calvin, *Calvin's Commentaries*, vol. XXI, trans. by William Pringle (Grand Rapids: Baker Book House, reprint ed. 1979), 186.

of Satan, who claim to be Jews though they are not, but are liars—I will make them come and fall down at your feet and acknowledge that I have loved you" (Rev 3:9). The resurrected Christ is dealing with those who continued saying they were God's people when they are in fact of Satan. It is similar to when He walked on the earth and told the leaders of the synagogue they were of their father, the Devil (John 8:44). He is saying that His followers are the true believers in Smyrna. They are the ones He loves and He will make those who claim to be Jews but are not, to come and fall down and acknowledge it.

We are told by John in the first chapter of Revelation that Jesus has "freed us from our sins and made us to be a kingdom and priest to serve His God and Father …" (Rev 1:5-6). To be made a priest is to be made an Israelite. Later when John sees into heaven he gets a glimpse of these redeemed people. The twenty-four elders fall down and worship with the four living creatures before the Lamb and sing a new song declaring:

You are worthy to take the scroll and open its seals, because you were slain, and with your blood you purchased for God persons from every tribe and language and people and nation. You have made them to be a kingdom and priest to serve our God, and they will reign on the earth. (Rev 5:9-10)

This is a picture of the redeemed called the Church. They are out of every tribe, language, people, and nation. These are the people of God.

The Seed of Abraham
Discussion Questions

1. What is the meaning of the name of Israel?

2. In the New Testament, the scripture speaks of two types of Israel. What are they?

3. What verse in the Bible says that all who are Israel are not Israel?

4. According to Galatians 3:6-9, who are the sons of Abraham?

5. Why does Paul point out that the promise was made to Abraham's "seed" (singular) and not to his seeds" (plural)?

6. According to Ephesians 3:2-6, what is the mystery of God?

7. The Greek word for church is *ekklessia*. What does this term mean?

8. The wall of separation between what two people has been torn down?

9. Read Ephesians 2:11-19 from several different translations and give a summary of what is being said.

CHAPTER 2

Promise by Faith or Race?

Is the promise of Abraham continued through race or faith? Are the children of Abraham determined by a percentage of human blood or Christ's blood? Are the natural descendants of Abraham included in the promise because they are born into a particular line? Or are the promises according to their faith? This question is the center of the much of Paul the apostle's teaching. Jesus addressed this question with the Jews of His day, as it did with the apostles in the early Church.

One Family

One such conflict became apparent when Jesus gave the parable concerning the Kingdom of God. He spoke to the Pharisees and chief priests and said the kingdom would be taken from them and given to another that would bear true fruit. He spoke of taking the kingdom from *natural Israel* and giving it to another, *spiritual Israel*, thus making them the *true Israel* of God. The Pharisees and chief priests understood He was talking about them and wanted to have him arrested.

Jesus said:

Therefore I tell you that the kingdom of God will be taken away from you and given to a people who will produce its fruit. He who falls on this stone will be broken to pieces, but he on whom it falls will be crushed." When the chief priests and the Pharisees heard Jesus' parables, they knew he was talking about them. They looked for a way to arrest him, but they were afraid of the crowd because the people held that he was a prophet. (Matt. 21:43-46)

Who are those who will produce its fruit that Jesus was talking about? Peter, the apostle, explains who the people are when he calls it a holy nation. He explains it is a priesthood and a chosen people: "But you are a chosen generation, a royal priesthood, a holy nation, His own special people, that you may proclaim the praises of Him who called you out of darkness into His marvelous light " (1 Peter 2:9). These are the same ones spoken about in the Book of Revelation as a kingdom and priest to serve God (Rev 1:6).

When Paul preached to the Jerusalem mob in Acts 21 and 22, they listened to him until he mentioned that he was sent to the Gentiles. Once he made that declaration, they "raised their voices and said, 'Away with such a fellow from the earth, for he is not fit to live!' Then they cried out and tore off their clothes and threw dust into the air'" (Acts 22:21-23). To think that God was including anyone other than the natural Jew was highly offensive to them and was rejected.

The same conflict continues today. Rather than accept the fact that God has "one family," many see the promise divided between two peoples. Dispensationalism teaches that God has the covenant with the natural Jew based upon Abraham's promise, and Christians have a covenant only through the Jews. It is true that our heritage is in the Jews who had faith in the coming Christ. We were grafted into the promise through Christ. However, Hal Lindsey, author of *The Late Great Planet Earth,* has said, "Christians have gotten in on the credit card of the Jews." Meaning the Church is not in covenant with Christ, but only through the natural Jew. He misses the fact the Church is the promise of God fulfilled in Christ. But for the Dispensationalist, there remains a future fulfillment of this promise to national Israel ruling the world with the Messiah as king. According to the Dispensationalist the Church and Israel remain separated even through eternity.

Dispensationalists' View

To reach this conclusion, Dispensationalists have asserted that Judaism and Christianity are two permanently separate religions, approved by God, with a different plan of salvation. Quoting, L.S. Chafer, a well-known Dispensationalist, Loraine Boettner in his book, *The Millennium,* writes,

> *The Bible distinguishes between God's consistent and eternal earthly purposes, which is the substance of Judaism; and His consistent and eternal heavenly purpose, which is the substance of Christianity, and it is as illogical and fanciful to contend that Judaism and Christianity ever merge as it would be to contend that heaven and earth cease to exist as separate spheres.[7]*

Since Dispensationalism demands that the two are separate and not made one in Christ, there must be two different gospels preached. C.I. Scofield, author of the *Scofield Reference Bible,* explains the dichotomy by "drawing a contrast between what is termed the 'The Gospel of the Kingdom' and the 'The Gospel of the

---

[7] Loraine Boettner, *The Millennium* (Phillipsburg, NJ: Presbyterian and Reformed Publishing, 1957) 303.

Grace of God.'" Boettner quotes Scofield concerning the Gospel of the Kingdom as saying,

> *"This good news that God proposes to set up on the earth, in fulfillment of the Davidic covenant (2 Sam 7:16) a kingdom, political, spiritual, Israelitish, universal, over which God's Son, David's heir, shall be King, and which shall be for one thousand years, the manifestation of the righteousness of God in human affairs." Since there are two separate bodies of faithful, Jews and Christians, Scofield goes on to say there are "two preachings of this Gospel, …one past, beginning with the ministry of John the Baptist, continued by our Lord and His disciples, and ending with the Jewish rejection of the King. The other is yet future (Matt. 24:14), during the great tribulation, and immediately preceding the coming of the King of glory."[8]*

Dispensationalism teaches that when Jesus came to this earth, his intent was to set up the Davidic kingdom and because the Jews rejected Christ, it was postponed for the future. Therefore, there must be another opportunity for Jews to be saved during the tribulation and millennium. They believe the "gospel of the grace of God" was offered to the Church, and the kingdom teaching is for the future millennium reign for the Jews. Boettner goes on to explain Scofield's reasoning.

> *"The contrast between these two gospels is brought out by the statement that the Sermon on the Mount, which belongs to the Gospel of the Kingdom, is said to be not the ideal standard for living in this present age, but to be the 'constitution' for the kingdom of heaven which was offered to the Jews at the first advent. The Sermon on the Mount is said to be 'pure law'; and 'there is not a*

---

[8] Boettner, 305-306.

ray of grace in it, nor a drop of blood.' This means that the Gospel of the Kingdom as it was offered does not require nor involve the Cross. The Kingdom as it was offered to the Jews, and as it is to be set up in the Millennium, is a reign of law, not of grace."[9]

Dispensationalism holds that since the promise was made forever, those who claim to be Jews today maintain a covenant through their father Abraham that is in effect beyond and outside the gospel age. It is true, the promise was made forever. However, it is how you view the fulfillment of that promise that determines the place for natural Israel in the course of eschatology.

This was the very subject that Christ and Paul, the apostle, dealt with in the Gospels and epistles. When Abraham received the promise, God was making it to Christ in Abraham. *Gil's Exposition of the Entire Bible* gives a clear explanation:

"And in thee shall all families of the earth be blessed; that is, in his seed, as in Genesis 22:18 and which is interpreted of Christ, Acts 3:25 meaning not every individual of all the families or nations of the earth; but that as many as believe in Christ, of all nations, are blessed in him; and that whoever of them are blessed, they are blessed and only blessed in him, and that they are blessed for his sake with all spiritual blessings."

Christ was in Abraham's loins when God made a covenant with him. It was to Abraham's seed that the promise was made. That is exactly what Paul is making clear in Galatians, when he says: "Even as Abraham believed God, and it was accounted to him for righteousness. Know ye therefore that they which are of faith, the same are the children of Abraham" (Gal 3:67).

---

[9] Boettner, 306.

The promise to Abraham was made to His "seed" and not to His "seeds." This point becomes particularly important to Paul, the apostle. Paul said that it was not to the seeds, but singularly to the seed that the promise was made. He wrote: "Now to Abraham and his seed were the promises made. He saith not, And to seeds, as of many; but as of one, And to thy seed, which is Christ" (Gal 3:16). The reason Paul makes this an emphasis is to show that the Christ is the *Seed,* rather than the physical descendants of Israel. He shows the word *seed* is singular referring to Christ, not plural as to refer to the natural descendants. The reason Jews today miss the Messiah is because they see the promise as made to natural Israel as the seeds, rather than to Christ as THE SEED. Dispensationalists make this same mistake, totally missing the apostolic message of the church.

Types, Shadows, and Patterns

Paul, the apostle, taught the opposite. He wrote, "there is neither Jew nor Gentile, but a new creation as one new body." All believers are seen as the children of Abraham. Centuries ahead, God showed Abraham the day that Christ would first come and that the covenant would be for all nations and families of the earth. Jesus said, "Your father Abraham rejoiced to see My day, and he saw it and was glad" (John 8:56). We are told that the gospel was preached to Abraham. That explains why Abraham was willing to offer Isaac on the altar, because he had seen the promise of the Messiah. Paul wrote: "And the scripture foreseeing that God would justify the nations by faith, preached the gospel to Abraham beforehand saying, 'In you all the nations shall be blessed'" (Gal 3:8). Paul continues to write, "… those who are of faith are blessed with believing Abraham" (Gal 3:9).

Whether Jew or Gentiles, all who have faith in Jesus Christ are the true Israel of God. Paul wrote, "For in Christ Jesus neither circumcision nor uncircumcision avails anything, but a new creation. And as many as walk according to this rule, peace and mercy be upon them, and upon the Israel of God" (Gal 6:15, 16).

The physical temple, priesthood, and sacrifices were merely types and symbols of the spiritual realities we now have in Christ. All the natural things of the Old Testament were but a shadow of the real under the better covenant. God spoke of how He would bring His people to be one by engrafting the *wild olive branches* of Gentiles, and the *cut-off branches* of Jews, through faith in the same promise of Abraham. That promise was Christ. We are shown a picture of a righteous remnant of faithful Jewish believers in the Messiah, grafted back into God's Olive Tree along with Gentile believers to form one Olive Tree in Christ.

> *And if some of the branches were broken off, and you, being a wild olive tree, were grafted in among them, and with them became a partaker of the root and fatness of the olive tree, do not boast against the branches. But if you do boast, remember that you do not support the root, but the root supports you. You will say then, "Branches were broken off that I might be grafted in." Well said. Because of unbelief they were broken off, and you stand by faith. Do not be haughty, but fear. For if God did not spare the natural branches, He may not spare you either. Therefore, consider the goodness and severity of God: on those who fell, severity; but toward you, goodness, if you continue in His goodness. Otherwise you also will be cut off. And they also, if they do not continue in unbelief, will be grafted in, for God is able to graft them in again.* (Rom. 11:17-23)

Jesus told his disciples from the very beginning there were those who were not natural descendants of Abraham, yet they would hear His voice and be one flock with one shepherd. He spoke of the

Gentiles when he said, "And other sheep I have which are not of this fold; them also I must bring, and they will hear My voice; and there will be one flock and one shepherd" (John 10:16).

Israel Fulfilled

Paul begins Chapter 11 of Romans identifying with natural Israel and declaring those who have been saved are not cast out; therefore, all of Israel has not been lost. He wrote, "Has God cast away His people? Certainly not! For I also am an Israelite, of the seed of Abraham of the tribe of Benjamin. God has not cast away His people whom He foreknew" (Rom. 11:1, 2a). Paul goes on to speak of that remnant that remained and chosen by grace of which he belonged (Rom. 11:6). It was by grace that God loved the patriarchs, and through election brought forth the true Israel in faith even as a remnant (Rom. 11:28). Paul tells us that what natural Israel so earnestly sought to obtain, it did not, but the elect did, and the others were hardened (Rom. 11:7). He is telling us that not all of Israel was cut off, only the unbelieving. Those who believe are of the elect. God has always had a people of faith.

This chapter of Romans is very crucial in understanding, "Who is the Israel of God?" As we have seen, Paul spends the two previous chapters emphasizing the following: "They are not all Israel who are of Israel, nor are they all children because they are the seed of Abraham" (Rom. 9:6, 7). He draws upon the Old Testament prophet Isaiah, declaring, "Though the number of children of Israel be as the sand of the sea, the remnant will be saved" (Rom. 9:27).

Paul travails over his desire to see his brethren saved.

Brethren, my heart's desire and prayer to God for Israel is that they may be saved. For I bear them witness that they have a zeal for God, but not according to knowledge. For they, being ignorant of

42

God's righteousness, and seeking to establish their own righteousness, have not submitted to the righteousness of God. (Rom. 10:13)

Just when you might think Paul is saying there will be no Israel, he clarifies his thoughts by announcing: "At this present time there is a remnant according to the election of grace" (Rom. 11:5). God has always had a plan to have "a people" that He can call His. He started with Adam. After man's fall in Adam, there was a promise given to Abraham of the last Adam, Christ Jesus. He came to the earth to redeem mankind and bring forth this people. Even in the garden, we see the first proclamation of that promise that Christ would come to fulfill the purpose of God. In Genesis it says, "And I will put enmity between you and the woman, and between your seed and her seed; it shall bruise your head, and you shall bruise his heel" (Gen. 3:15). This promise of the covenant was revealed to Abraham, which was, in reality to Christ, His SEED (Gal 3:16). Jesus was seen as the last Adam, the life-giving spirit, thus the spiritual came after the first Adam, which was natural. Paul explains, "And so it is written, 'The first man, Adam, became a living being.' The last Adam became a life giving spirit. However, the spiritual is not first, but the natural, and afterward the spiritual" (1 Cor. 15:45-46).

Paul goes on to clarify for this promise to be fulfilled as the Israel of God both the natural branches, and the wild olive tree, are grafted into the same root. This was his message to the Galatians: "For in Christ Jesus neither circumcision nor uncircumcision avails anything, but a new creation. . ." (Gal. 6:15). Paul is actually saying that the new birth in Christ makes you an Israelite, not circumcision or uncircumcision, which is the sign of belonging to natural Israel. By Paul's own words, we see that those of faith are the seed of Abraham and thus the *Israel of God.*

How Natural Israel Will be Saved

Another issue in understanding the fulfillment of Israel, has to do with the verses in Romans 11 that indicate that all of natural Israel will be saved.

> *For if God did not spare the natural branches, He may not spare you either. Therefore consider the goodness and severity of God: on those who fell, severity; but toward you, goodness, if you continue in His goodness. Otherwise you also will be cut off. And they also, if they do not continue in unbelief, will be grafted in, for God is able to graft them in again. For if you were cut out of the olive tree which is wild by nature, and were grafted contrary to nature into a cultivated olive tree, how much more will these, who are natural branches, be grafted into their own olive tree? For I do not desire, brethren, that you should be ignorant of this mystery, lest you should be wise in your own opinion, that blindness in part has happened to Israel until the fullness of the Gentiles has come in.* **And so all Israel will be saved,** *as it is written: "The Deliverer will come out of Zion, and He will turn away ungodliness from Jacob."* (Rom. 11:21-26) (Emphasis mine.)

Paul wrote to the Romans before the Roman armies invaded Jerusalem, speaking of the fullness of the Gentiles, "And so all Israel will be saved, as it is written: "The Deliverer will come out of Zion, and He will turn away ungodliness from Jacob" (Rom. 11:21-26). In this passage, he describes "how" Israel was to be saved, not "when" Israel would be saved. The word "so" according to *The Webster Dictionary* defines the word "as like manner." Paul is telling us "how" all of Israel will be saved. This explains how Gentiles and Jews are one. It happens by the grafting in of the wild olive branches and bringing back to life the natural branches who abide not in unbelief. Both Jew and Gentile, in Christ Jesus, who is the Root, make up this Israel of God. Paul quotes Isaiah in verse 27, "For this is My covenant with them, when I take away their sins" (Rom 11:27). It is in Jesus that sins are taken away, for both Jew and Gentile. This is how *all Israel* is saved. There is no other way to be saved.

Now we can understand Galatians 6:14-16, and why Paul would not boast in his natural heritage, but only in Christ:

> *May I never boast except in the cross of our Lord Jesus Christ, through which the world has been crucified to me, and I to the world. Neither circumcision nor uncircumcision means anything; what counts is the new creation." Peace and mercy to all who follow this rule—to the Israel of God.*

The above passage in Romans 11, is often used by Dispensationalists to show that in the future all of Israel will be saved in a day. Isaiah is quoted to support that thought:

> *Who has heard such a thing? Who has seen such things? Shall the earth be made to give birth in one day? Or shall a nation be born at once? For as soon as Zion was in labor, she gave birth to her children.* (Isa. 66:8)

Some say that Isaiah is referring to this time when a nation is born in a day, that this is none other than modern-day Jews. They teach that someday in the future there will be a revival and the Jews will all become Christians in a day. Some Dispensationalists use Isaiah 66 to point to May 14, 1948, the day in which the British Mandate over Palestine expired, the *Jewish People's Council* gathered at the Tel Aviv Museum, and declared the establishment of the State of Israel.

The nation that is brought forth in a day is actually the Church made up of all the families of the earth. The holy nation that Peter speaks of as a special people. This happened on the Day of Pentecost when Zion was in labor and gave birth to her children. It came forth in a day—Day of Pentecost.

Hardened Hearts

What does the Bible tell us about why natural Israel rejected Christ? The disciples asked that same question when they heard Jesus teaching in parables. Jesus quoted the prophet Isaiah and explained:

> *This is why I speak to them in parables: "Though seeing, they do not see; though hearing, they do not hear or understand. In them is fulfilled the prophecy of Isaiah: " 'You will be ever hearing but never understanding; you will be ever seeing but never perceiving. For this people's heart has become calloused; they hardly hear with their ears, and they have closed their eyes. Otherwise they might see with their eyes, hear with their ears, understand with their hearts and turn, and I would heal them.' But blessed are your eyes because they see, and your ears because they hear.* (Matt. 13:10-16)

Paul explains Israel had their hearts hardened until the fullness of the Gentiles has come in. He writes, "For I do not desire, brethren, that you should be ignorant of this mystery, lest you should be wise in your own opinion, that blindness in part has happened to Israel until the fullness of the Gentiles has come in." (Rom. 11:25)

We know the *hardening* was to continue until the destruction of Jerusalem, because when Isaiah asked God how long they would be blinded he was told. The Prophet was told it would take place until the cities were laid waste and utterly forsaken, then a remnant called the holy seed would remain.

Make the heart of this people calloused; make their ears dull and close their eyes. Otherwise they might see with their eyes, hear with their ears, understand with their hearts, and turn and be healed." Then I said, "For how long, O Lord?" And he answered: "Until the cities lie ruined and without inhabitant, until the houses are left deserted and the fields ruined and ravaged, until the LORD has sent everyone far away and the land is utterly forsaken. And though a tenth remains in the land, it will again be laid waste. But as the terebinth and oak leave stumps when they are cut down, so the holy seed will be the stump in the land." (Isa 6:10-13)

The time of the Gentiles began when Israel and Judah came under captivity, first by the Assyrians and then by Babylon. In 586 B.C., when the Babylonians took Judah captive, they came under Gentile rule. After the Babylonians, the Medo-Persians came, and then Greece and Rome. It was during this time period of the Roman armies that the time of the Gentiles was fulfilled. When the final destruction of Jerusalem was finished, then the Jews would as Jesus said, "Fill up, then, the measure of your fathers' guilt" (Matt 23:32). According to Luke 21:24, the times of the Gentiles were fulfilled in the destruction of Jerusalem as declared by Jesus in the Olivet discourse. Jesus said, "And they will fall by the edge of the sword, and be led away captive into all nations. And Jerusalem will be trampled by Gentiles until the times of the Gentiles are fulfilled."

They were led away captive and many killed by the sword. Josephus, the Jewish historian, says that more than a million Jews lost their lives and nearly one hundred thousand were led away captive. The Roman armies of 70 AD, and the destruction of Jerusalem in fulfillment to Jesus' prophecy in Luke 21:6, reveal the times of the Gentiles being fulfilled.

There are those who call this teaching "replacement theology." That label is intended to indicate anti-Semitism, accusing anyone who would teach these things must be trying to replace Israel. That is not any more accurate than for it to be said Dispensationalism is "genetic theology," that someone is saved by the amount of bloodline they have. What is offered in this book is "fulfillment theology." Paul the apostle, did not teach replacement theology, but a fulfillment of all the prophets declared. Jesus and the cross did not replace anything, but rather fulfilled everything spoken by the prophets and declared in the law. Jesus is the center of the plan of God for the ages. We are to have a healthy love for the patriarchs who brought forth the Messiah. Without the Jewish patriarchs, we as Gentiles would never have heard of the gospel; therefore, we are forever humble and grateful. The gospel came to the Jews first and then the Gentiles.

In John Hagee's book, *Beginning of the End, The Assassination of Yitzhak Rabin and the Coming Antichrist,* he writes of Israel's future declaring that Psalm 89:28-34 was proof that even though natural Israel had broken covenant, that God had given the promises to natural Israel forever.[10]

> *I will maintain my love to him forever, and my covenant with him will never fail. I will establish his line forever, his throne as long as the heavens endure. "If his sons forsake my law and do not follow my statutes, if they violate my decrees and fail to keep my commands, I will punish their sin with the rod, their iniquity with flogging; but I will not take my love from him, nor will I ever betray my faithfulness. I will not violate my covenant or alter what my lips have uttered.* (Ps. 89:28-34)

---

[10] John Hagee, Beginning of the End, *The Assassination of Yitzhak Rabin and the Coming Antichrist* (Nashville, TN: Thomas Nelson Publishers, 1996) 30.

Ratified Covenant

Once again, it is about Christ. This passage used by Hagee as proof text that the promise was to natural Israel, is not about the natural seeds but about the Seed, Jesus Christ. This Messianic prophecy is speaking of Christ. Charles Spurgeon explains this is Jesus:

> *The kings of David's line needed mercy, and mercy prevented their house from utterly perishing until the Son of Mary came. He needs no mercy for himself, but he is a representative man, and the mercy of God is required for those who are in him: for such mercy is kept forever. And my covenant shall stand fast with him. With Jesus, the covenant is ratified both by blood of sacrifice and by oath of God, it cannot be cancelled or altered, but is an eternal verity, resting upon the veracity of one who cannot lie.*[11]

The promise in Psalm 89 was forever, and was to Christ. The promise to Abraham was, "And I will give unto you, and to your seed after you… all the land of Canaan for an everlasting possession" (Gen 17:8). Paul tells us,

> *For the promise that he should be heir of the world, was not to Abraham, or to his seed through the law, but through the righteousness of faith. For if they which are of the law be heirs, faith is made void, and the promise made of none effect.* (Rom. 4:13, 14)

John Bray, in his book *Israel in Bible Prophecy*, explains the fulfillment of the promise in reference to the above verse:

> *This plainly says that the promise or covenant was not for earthly Israel ("They which are of the law"). This was because the promise included more than just land. Earthly Israel did inherit the*

---

[11] Charles H. Spurgeon, *The Treasury of David*, Psalm 89.

land as mentioned (Joshua 21:44, 46; Nehemiah 9:8), and no one can rightly say they did not possess exactly what God promised to them, even though later they were dispossessed of the land. But the covenant went beyond the physical land. Abraham surely understood this, and did not pay much attention to the earthly part of things, but rather looked for a city which had foundations whose builder and maker is God (see Heb. 11:10 and Gen 13:15-17). God's promise of the spiritual blessings were intended to be fulfilled in spiritual Israel (the true seed).[12]

The Church has been understood to be the people of God throughout church history, and still is today even among the Orthodox Church. "The term 'people of God' in the Orthodox Church is understood as members of the body of Christ and as the pleroma (fullness) of the Church, the 'Israel of God,' the 'saints,' the 'elect,' the 'chosen race,' and the 'royal priesthood.'"[13]

Many in the Orthodox Church understood the meaning of Israel in Scripture. Georges Florovsky, a Russian of the Orthodox Church, is just one of many. He made this clear in the following statement:

The first followers of Jesus in the "days of His flesh," were not isolated individuals engaged in their private quest for truth. They were Israelites regular members of an established and instituted Community of the "Chosen People" of God ... Indeed; a "Church" already existed when Jesus began His ministry. It was Israel, the People of the Covenant... The existing Covenant was the constant background of His preaching. The Sermon on the Mount was addressed not to an occasional crowd of accidental listeners, but rather to an "inner circle" of those who were

---

[12] John L. Bray, *Israel in Bible Prophecy* (Lakeland, FL: John L. Bray Ministries, Inc, 1983) 67.

[13] Vassiliades, "New Testament Ecclesiological Perspectives on Laity", p.348. Acts 9:31,41; 26:19; Gal. 6:16; Rom. 1:7; 8:27, 33; 12:13; 15:25; Col. 3:12; 1 Peter 2:9.

already following Jesus… "The Little Flock" that the community which Jesus had gathered around Himself was, in fact, the faithful "Remnant" of Israel, a reconstituted People of God… Each person had to respond individually by an act of personal faith. This personal commitment of faith, however, incorporated the believer into the Community. And this remained forever the pattern of Christian existence: one should believe and confess, and then he is baptized, baptized into the Body.[14]

As we look at God's plan for the ages, it becomes increasingly clear that His people called Israel, are made up of *those who have faith in God through Christ*. Abraham was considered righteous because he believed God when the gospel was preached to him. The promise to Abraham was that his seed would be as the sands of the sea and the stars of the sky, impossible for him to count. The only way this could be fulfilled was for Jesus to come as the Seed. For the promise to be as the sands of the sea and the stars of the sky, it must move beyond natural Israel to the fulfillment of the promise in Christ. Natural Israel can be counted; the saints in Christ are too numerous to count. If the gospel was preached to Abraham, then he must have been told of the Seed, Christ Jesus. Abraham, like David, was a prophet and able to see ahead to Christ, as the scripture declares: "Therefore, being a prophet, and knowing that God had sworn with an oath to him that the fruit of his body, according to the flesh, He would raise up the Christ to sit on his throne" (Acts 2:30). These patriarchs, like Moses, saw Him who was invisible. The Christ and the plan of God was declared through the gospel preached to Abraham.

---

[14] Georges Florovsky, *Worship and Everyday Life: An Eastern Orthodox View*, Studia Patristica, vol. 2 (1963), 266.

Promise by Faith or Race?
Discussion Questions

1. When Jesus said that He would take the kingdom from the natural Jews and give it to a nation that would bring forth the fruit of righteousness, who is this nation that would bring forth the fruit (1 Peter 2:9)?

2. What was the response of the Jews when Paul said that he was being sent to the Gentiles (Acts 21:21-23)?

3. Give the scripture that proves that Abraham heard the gospel in his day.

4. According to Galatians 6:15-16, who are the Israel of God?

5. When Jesus spoke to His disciples He referred to "sheep who were not of this fold." Who are these sheep (John 10:16)? _____

6. According to Romans 11:5, what has determined the salvation of the remnant?

7. In Romans 11:26, Paul says, "And so all Israel will be saved..." If the word "so" is an adverb meaning in like manner, does it speak to "when" or "how?"

CHAPTER 3

Inauguration of the Kingdom

The Reign of God

When did the kingdom of God begin? In the overall view, there never has been a time when the kingdom of God did not exist. When we speak of the kingdom of God we simply refer to the reign of God over and above all things. The Psalmist declares, "The Lord reigns, he is robed in majesty; the Lord is robed in majesty and armed with strength; indeed, the world is established, firm and secure. Your throne was established long ago you are from eternity" (Ps. 93:1, 2).

Even though we can say the reign of God has always existed, Christ was sent to establish His Day of the kingdom. The church, or body of Christ in the earth, has become the instrument of that kingdom under the new covenant. In the Old Testament, the kingdom of God on the earth was seen in natural Israel under the throne of David and his descendants. Once again, as a shadow, it pointed to what was to come. The Davidic kingdom was a preview of what Christ was to inaugurate as the fruit of David's loins. Peter, as a

New Testament apostle, gives us the understanding that David saw ahead to Christ's day and spoke of the resurrection and ascension as being the day that Christ was placed as King of Kings. Peter makes the connection for us in his message on the Day of Pentecost. He wanted all to hear that Jesus was placed upon the throne of David in the resurrection and the ascension.

> *Men and brethren, let me freely speak unto you of the patriarch David, that he is both dead and buried, and his sepulchre is with us unto this day. Therefore, being a prophet, and knowing that God had sworn with an oath to him, that of the fruit of his loins, according to the flesh, he would raise up Christ to sit on his throne; He seeing this before spake of the resurrection of Christ, that his soul was not left in hell, neither his flesh did see corruption. This Jesus hath God raised up, whereof we all are witnesses. Therefore being by the right hand of God exalted, and having received of the Father the promise of the Holy Ghost, he hath shed forth this, which ye now see and hear.* (Acts 2:29-33)

Peter was boldly declaring that the inauguration of the kingdom of Christ had come. The day of Pentecost was proof to the Jew and the world, that Christ was seated on the throne of David. Up to this day, Jesus and John the Baptist had declared the kingdom of God was *at hand.* However, after the resurrection, Jesus no longer declared the kingdom of God was at hand; rather, He taught them *concerning* the kingdom. Why? Because it was here and present. The day of Pentecost was the evidence that Christ sat on his throne as was promised to David. That is why after the resurrection, and before the Day of Pentecost, Jesus spent time teaching them about the kingdom:

> *Until the day in which he was taken up, after that he, through the Holy Ghost, had given commandments unto the apostles*

whom he had chosen: To whom also he showed himself alive after his passion by many infallible proofs, being seen of them forty days, and speaking of the things pertaining to the kingdom of God. (Acts 1:2, 3)

The apostles did the same, declaring that Christ was the promised Messiah to sit upon His throne according to the prophets.

And we declare unto you glad tidings, how that the promise which was made unto the fathers, God hath fulfilled the same unto us their children, in that he hath raised up Jesus again; as it is also written in the second psalm, Thou art my Son, this day have I begotten thee. (Acts 13:32, 33)

Paul's message was the gospel of the kingdom. Luke writes of Paul, "Preaching the kingdom of God, and teaching those things which concern the Lord Jesus Christ, with all confidence, no man forbidding him" (Acts 28:31). We see the kingdom brought forth by Christ. Jesus is worshiped in the Book of Revelation as one who was worthy to take the scroll and to open its seals, because he was slain and by His blood He purchased for God people from every tribe, language, and nation. He made them to be a kingdom and priest to serve God (Rev 5:9-10).

A Future Kingdom?

Dispensationalists teach that the kingdom is still in the future. They insist that the throne of David has been vacated for the past 2,500 years. Authors Curtis Crenshaw and Grover Gunn, quote Lewis Sperry Chafer in their book *Dispensationalism Today, Yesterday, and Tomorrow*, saying, "the throne of David is precisely what David believed it to be, an earthly institution which has never been, nor will it ever be, in heaven."[15] They have relegated this to a future time that Christ will sit upon David's throne here on the earth in the city of Jerusalem. However, the apostles tell us that Jesus was made both Lord and Christ, meaning He has been crowned King of Kings and Lord of Lords and seated on the throne of David at the ascension.

> *For David is not ascended into the heavens: but he saith himself, The LORD said unto my Lord, Sit thou on my right hand, until I make thy foes thy footstool. Therefore, let all the house of Israel know assuredly that God hath made that same Jesus, whom ye have crucified, both Lord and Christ.* (Acts 2:34-36)

With Christ sitting on the throne now, there cannot be a future time when Christ will have more power or authority than He was given at the resurrection. Paul describes His authority as above every name.

> *...when He raised him from the dead, and set him at His own right hand in the heavenly places, far above all principality, and power, and might, and dominion, and every name that is named, not only in this world, but also in that which is to come: And hath put all things under his feet, and gave him to be the head over all things to the church...* (Eph. 1:20-22)

When Jesus said, "All authority has been given to Me in heaven and on earth..." (Matt 28:18), He was proclaiming His Kingship not only in heaven but on the earth. There is no indication from Jesus that His rule over the nations of the earth was being postponed to a future time. On the contrary, His proclamation was the basis for commanding His followers to make disciples of all the nations. His kingdom and government will continue to increase, so there will be

---

[15] Curtis I. Crenshaw and Grover E. Gunn, III, *Dispensationalism Today, Yesterday, and Tomorrow* (Memphis, TN: Footstool Publishing, 1985) 342.

a fuller expression in the future, but we are not waiting for a future reign. His kingdom is present and increasing.

Right before his ascension into heaven, Jesus gave His disciples the command to receive the promise of the Father, the outpouring of the Holy Spirit. Knowing there was a connection with what the prophets had prophesied, they knew the kingdom of the Messiah was related to the outpouring of the Holy Spirit. They asked Him, "saying, Lord, wilt thou at this time restore again the kingdom to Israel?" (Acts 1:6). It might seem to the casual observer that He was changing the subject, or ignoring their request, when He answered, "It is not for you to know the times or the seasons, which the Father hath put in his own power" (Acts 1:7). But He did, in fact, answer the question directly by continuing with a response and told them "how" the kingdom would come, rather than "when" it would come. He said, "But you shall receive power when the Holy Spirit has come upon you; and you shall be witnesses to Me in Jerusalem, and in all Judea and Samaria, and to the end of the earth" (Acts 1:8). He was pointing out the fact that the kingdom is a spiritual kingdom, extended through the preaching of the gospel with the power of the Holy Spirit, beginning in Jerusalem and spreading to the ends of the earth.

His disciples were still looking for a national, political, and earthly kingdom. They had apparently interpreted the Old Testament prophets the way some still do today, coming to the conclusion that the Messiah's kingdom is to be a kingdom seen by natural observations. Jesus had addressed this in Luke 17:20, 21, speaking to the Pharisees before His disciples.

Now when He was asked by the Pharisees when the kingdom of God would come, He answered them and said, "The kingdom of

God does not come with observation; nor will they say, 'See here!'
or 'See there!' For indeed, the kingdom of God is within you."

The Spiritual Kingdom

Paul, the apostle, tells us this is a spiritual kingdom when he writes, "the kingdom of God is... righteousness and peace and joy in the Holy Spirit" (Rom. 14:17). Paul states that Christ has delivered "us from the power of darkness and conveyed us into the kingdom of the Son of His love" (Col. 1:13).

In his writings to the Church in Corinth, Paul explains the connection with the resurrection of Christ and His present reign declaring, "He must reign" until His all enemies are placed under His feet. The Church is His body and we are His feet. This reign continues from the time of His resurrection until the last day resurrection of us all. We know this continues until then, because the last enemy to be defeated is death. That defeat will finally take place in the literal resurrection. The work Christ did in His death, burial, and resurrection becomes a reality for our bodies. Until then, it is called the Messiah's Day or the kingdom of Christ. When this comes to an end He turns it over to the Father.

But each in turn: Christ, the firstfruits; then, when he comes,
those who belong to him. Then the end will come, when he
hands over the kingdom to God the Father after he has destroyed
all dominion, authority and power. For he must reign until he
has put all his enemies under his feet. The last enemy to be
destroyed is death. For he "has put everything under his feet."
Now when it says that "everything" has been put under him, it
is clear that this does not include God himself, who put every-
thing under Christ. When he has done this, then the Son himself

will be made subject to him who put everything under him, so that God may be all in all. (1 Cor. 15:23-28)

The Gathering of Israel into His Kingdom

This kingdom is not only a spiritual kingdom, but we find out it is the fulfillment of the scriptures concerning the gathering of Israel. The apostles of the first-generation Christians saw their purpose connected to the time of Christ's first advent. They knew the prophet Isaiah had declared that when the root of Jesse came, then He would bring in the day when the remnant would be gathered.

There shall come forth a Rod from the stem of Jesse, and a Branch shall grow out of his roots. The Spirit of the LORD shall rest upon Him... "And in that day there shall be a Root of Jesse, who shall stand as a banner to the people; for the Gentiles shall seek Him, and His resting place shall be glorious." It will come to pass in that day that the LORD will set His hand again the second time to recover the remnant of His people who are left... He will set up a banner for the nations, and will assemble the outcasts of Israel, and gather together the dispersed of Judah from the four corners of the earth. (Isa. 11:1; 10-12)

If we believe the Bible does not contain wasted or empty words, then we must consider statements like James makes when he writes, "To the twelve tribes which are scattered abroad: 'Greetings'" (James 1:1). James apparently saw himself writing to the believing remnant as a fulfillment of prophecy. Notice, he does not mention anything about the "so-called" ten lost tribes of Israel, but rather sees the *believing Jews* as the twelve tribes. As we read further, we find Peter speaking almost the same words in addressing the church.

> *Peter, an apostle of Jesus Christ, To the pilgrims of the Disper-sion in Pontus, Galatia, Cappadocia, Asia, and Bithynia, elect according to the foreknowledge of God the Father, in sanctifica-tion of the Spirit, for obedience and sprinkling of the blood of Jesus Christ: Grace to you and peace be multiplied.* (1 Pet.1:1, 2)

By the time Jesus had come on the scene at His first advent, the apostasy of the Jews had grown to such a degree that few even believed. This was the remnant the prophet Isaiah spoke of. He saw them as scattered abroad without a shepherd. Matthew wrote, "But when He saw the multitudes, He was moved with compassion for them, because they were weary and scattered, like sheep having no shepherd" (*Matt 9:36*).

The Jews of Jesus' day had gone so far away from the truth of the law, they had turned their faith into traditions that set aside the commandments of God. In their apostasy, they had added to the law of God through the Talmud, and made the commandments of God void by their own traditions. Jesus said:

> *And in vain they worship Me, teaching as doctrines the com-mandments of men. "For laying aside the commandment of God, you hold the tradition of men, the washing of pitchers and cups, and many other such things you do." And He said to them, "All too well you reject the commandment of God, that you may keep your tradition."* (Mark 7:7-9)

Those living in the time of John the Baptist were living in the dark days prophesied by Isaiah. They were waiting in darkness for the Light to come. For over 400 years, no prophetic word had come from the Lord. It was the darkest time in history. A world without Christ and without a fresh revelation from God. The prophet Isaiah declared:

Arise, shine; for your light has come! And the glory of the LORD is risen upon you. For behold, the darkness shall cover the earth, and deep darkness the people; but the LORD will arise over you, and His glory will be seen upon you. The Gentiles shall come to your light, and kings to the brightness of your rising. (Isa. 60:1)3

John knew he was not the light, but that he had come to bear witness to the light, even as the prophet had declared. John writes:

In Him was life, and the life was the light of men. And the light shines in the darkness, and the darkness did not comprehend it. There was a man sent from God, whose name was John. This man came for a witness, to bear witness of the Light, that all through him might believe. He was not that Light, but was sent to bear witness of that Light. That was the true Light which gives light to every man coming into the world. (John1:49)

Those who believed were baptized by John unto repentance in preparation for the way of the Lord, who was bringing in the kingdom of the Messiah. Not all of Israel were cut off, as Paul the apostle said that he himself was an Israelite, a descendant of Abraham from the tribe of Benjamin (Rom. 11:1). The first ten years of the gospel, all those who belonged to the believing remnant were all natural descendants of the house of Israel until Acts 10. The Church began as Jewish believers in Christ. Then the door of the kingdom was opened to the Gentiles beginning at Cornelius' house.

Now that they had received the Holy Spirit and understood, they could rejoice in what Jesus said. Jesus had told them that some of the natural Jews were blinded, but others were given the blessing to see and hear. Here in this passage Jesus explains that some of the natural Jews were blinded in part, while others like His disciples were given to see:

...It has been given to you to know the mysteries of the kingdom of heaven, but to them it has not been given. But blessed are your eyes for they see, and your ears for they hear; for assuredly, I say to you that many prophets and righteous men desired to see what you see, and did not see it, and to hear what you hear, and did not hear it. (Matt. 13:11, 16, 17)

The early church apostles knew that by preaching the gospel they were bringing an opportunity for the Jews, who were of the elect, to believe and be gathered into Christ's fold. That is why Peter and John and the other apostles spoke to the men of Israel. They spoke to the Jews and declared that the miracles done by the power of the Holy Spirit were a testimony of the risen Lord. Those who believed were gathered into Israel but those who rejected the Messiah were not made of the flock.

The gathering of Israel began with the preaching of the gospel to the Jews of the first century. It soon included Gentiles from the time of Acts 10. If the promise was for Abraham's seed to be innumerable, then it would require Jesus opening the door to all the nations of the world. This would be in keeping with the promise made to Abraham that he would be the father of many nations, and his Seed would bless the nations.

Jesus, talking about the growth of the Kingdom of God, said it this way, "It is like leaven, which a woman took and hid in three measures of meal till it was all leavened" (Luke 13:21). In other words, it filled the whole lump. Daniel's interpretation of Nebuchadnezzar's dream revealed the Kingdom of God would be like a "stone cut without hands... and the stone that struck the image became a great mountain and filled the whole earth" (Dan. 2:34, 35).

When you consider the number who have believed in Christ over the centuries, and now add to that number of those who are coming into the Kingdom today, you have a mass of people "as the sands of the sea and the stars of heaven."

What started as a few hundred believers in Christ's day has become billions of followers. *The U.S. Center for World Mission* estimated in 1997 that Christianity's total number of adherents is growing at about 2.3% annually. This is approximately equal to the growth rate of the world's population. Nearly thirty years ago, I heard Loren Cunningham, founder of *Youth with a Mission*, give some interesting information about the growth of Christianity over the centuries. He was quoting Barnett Institute when he said, "In Paul's day during the first century, there was only one believer for every 360 people. After 1,000 years of preaching the gospel, there was still only one believer for every 270 people. In 1900, there was one for every fifty one people; in 1950, one in twenty seven; in 1980, one in eleven; and in 1990, one believer for every seven people." Today, there is one in four and some claim one in three. What growth! It's amazing to see scripture fulfilled.

Inauguration of the Kingdom
Discussion Questions

1. Before the resurrection, John the Baptist and Jesus taught that the kingdom of God was at hand. After the resurrection and Pentecost, the apostles simply preached the kingdom. Identify a scripture where Paul preached the kingdom.

2. According to Acts 2:34-36, when was Jesus seated on the throne of David?

3. Jesus said that all authority in heaven and on _____ was given to him (Matt. 28:18).

4. When the disciples asked Jesus if this was the time He was going to restore again the kingdom to Israel, Jesus did not tell them when but _____ the kingdom was going to be restored.

5. What kind of kingdom did Jesus and the apostles speak about—a natural kingdom or a spiritual kingdom?

6. Name one Old Testament scripture that speaks of the gathering of Israel.

7. Name one New Testament scripture that speaks to all twelve tribes of Israel. _____

8. According to Isaiah 60:1-3 and John 1:4-9, what were the darkest days of history?

SECTION II

CHAPTER 4

The Olivet Discourse

Matthew 24, Mark 13, and Luke 21, are pivotal chapters in understanding God's dealing with natural Israel. The previous four chapters before Matthew 24, reveal Jesus giving outright warnings to Jerusalem and the whole nation, concerning the judgments that were about to come upon them.

The Setting of the Sign

Beginning in Matthew 20, Jesus declares that the kingdom of God is like a land owner who went out early in the morning to hire workers. Jesus tells of how the owner agreed with the workers to give a *denari* (normal day's wage), for a full day's work. They went into the field to work. At 9:00 in the morning, he made the same arrangement with other workers. Then again at noon and 3:00 in the afternoon. Finally, he hired workers at 5:00 p.m. with only one hour left to work. When the workers lined up at the end of the day to receive their pay they all received the same wage. The earlier workers were upset, but the land owner reminded them that he had kept his agreement.

Jesus was telling the natural Jews that even though they had been called for centuries, now those who are selected without the long history of works, will receive the same full blessings. He continues to make it clear that the first shall be last, and the last shall be first. He spoke of the Gentiles who would be considered last, yet they will be brought in and made a part of the kingdom by the grace of God after Jesus' death on the cross.

In Chapter 21 of Matthew, Jesus tells of the parable of the vineyard. He tells how the owner of the vineyard rented out the vineyard and then left. He later sent his servants to check on the vineyard. Those who had rented the vineyard refused to receive the servants and beat them. Finally, the owner sent his son. Those who were renting the vineyard killed the son in order to get the inheritance. Jesus explained that the owner would come and bring those renters to a "wretched" end and rent the vineyard to other renters who would bring forth produce. The Pharisees and chief priest of the Jews knew Jesus was talking about them as the first renters. Jesus declared that He would take the kingdom of God from them and give it to others who would produce righteousness. Jesus was speaking of the body of Christ who would bring forth fruit of righteousness.

In Chapter 22, Jesus tells them of another parable where a king gave a wedding feast for his son. He invited certain people to come to the wedding, but they ignored the invitation. The servants who had been sent to invite the guests to the feast were seized and mistreated and killed. Jesus compares these servants to the apostles and prophets sent to preach the gospel of the covenant to the Jews, but they would not receive it. Finally, in this parable, the king was enraged and sent his armies and destroyed those murderers and set their city on fire. Jesus is telling the Jews that judgment would come to their city of Jerusalem by the armies of Rome and bring great destruction and their city would be burned.

Stronger Warnings

In Chapter 23 of Matthew, the warnings get even stronger. Seven times in this chapter Jesus gives warnings to the Jews. Beginning in verse 13, He gives seven "woes" to the scribes and Pharisees. He warns them because they rejected John the Baptist. He warns them for religious posturing. He warns them for turning proselytes into sons of hell. He warns them about using loopholes to get around the law. He warns them about their priorities, and about being a hypocrite. He warns them about having no spiritual life; and finally, He warns them about pretending to support the prophets when, in fact, they are a witness against themselves, worthy of destruction.

With this final warning, He declares that *this generation* would receive the judgment for all the bloodshed of the righteous from Abel to Zechariah, the son of Berechiah. He says to Jerusalem that He wanted to gather their children to Himself, but they would not respond. Therefore, He declares that their house is left desolate. Notice, that no longer is it called "His house," but rather "your house." God was no longer dwelling in that house. God was in Christ, who was greater than the temple, yet He was being rejected by His own.

Notice how in each chapter leading up to Chapter 24 of Matthew, that the threats of judgment increase. It is in this setting, with these last warnings, that Jesus steps out of the temple. After so much talk of judgment, it seems as if the disciples attempted to get Jesus to redirect His attention from judgment to the beautiful temple. As they came out of the temple,

*His disciples came to Him to show Him the buildings of the temple. And Jesus said to them, 'Do you not see all these things? Assuredly, I say to you, not one stone shall be left **here** upon another, that shall not be thrown down.' Now as He sat on the Mount of Olives, the disciples came to Him privately, saying, 'Tell us, when will these things be? And what will be the sign of Your coming, and of the end of the age?'"* (Matt. 24: 2, 3) (Emphasis mine)

Instead of commenting on the beauty of temple, one final time Jesus speaks of judgment. This was shocking news to the disciples because of what the temple represented. They knew the temple was of God, built for God, and represented the headquarters of the earth for God's purposes. It would take God himself to providentially bring such judgment on the temple. They also understood something this catastrophic would mark the end of an age, and would have signs that would point to the coming judgment. They would have known that Jesus was speaking of that present temple and not some future rebuilt temple, because He references the temple "here."

The Gospel of Mark tells us that four disciples—Peter, James, John, and Andrew—asked Jesus privately, "Tell us, when will these things be? And what will be the sign when all these things will be fulfilled?" (Mark 13:4)

This Generation

In context of these passages, it was clear to the disciples that Jesus was referring to the generation in which they lived. He had told them in Matt. 23:36, that the judgment was coming on *this* generation. If Jesus had meant a future generation, He would have said *that* generation; rather He declared, "Assuredly, I say to you, all these things will come upon this generation."

This was not the first time Jesus had spoken about "this generation." When He was confronted by some of the scribes and Pharisees saying they wanted a sign, He identified them as *this generation* that would receive judgment:

Then some of the scribes and Pharisees answered, saying, "Teacher, we want to see a sign from You." But He answered and said to them, "An evil and adulterous generation seeks after a sign, and no sign will be given to it except the sign of the prophet Jonah. For as Jonah was three days and three nights in the belly of the great fish, so will the Son of Man be three days and three nights in the heart of the earth. The men of Nineveh will rise up in the judgment with **this generation** *and condemn it, because they repented at the preaching of Jonah; and indeed a greater than Jonah is here. The queen of the South will rise up in the judgment with* **this generation** *and condemn it, for she came from the ends of the earth to hear the wisdom of Solomon; and indeed a greater than Solomon is here."* (Matt. 12:38-42) (Emphasis mine)

Jesus went on to explain more concerning *their generation* and the wickedness it would become after He was gone. He describes apostate Israel as one filled with evil spirits and more wicked than it was at first.

When an unclean spirit goes out of a man, he goes through dry places, seeking rest, and finds none. Then he says, "I will return to my house from which I came." And when he comes, he finds it empty, swept, and put in order. Then he goes and takes with him seven other spirits more wicked than himself, and they enter and dwell there; and the last state of that man is worse than the *first. So shall it also be with **this wicked generation*** (Matt 12:43-45). (Emphasis mine)

Josephus gives us a testimony and confirmation of this generation of which our Lord spoke. Josephus, a Jewish historian living during the time of this generation, tells us,

As it were impossible to relate their enormities in detail, I shall briefly state that no other city ever endured similar calamities, and no generation ever existed more prolific in crime. They confessed themselves to be what they were slaves, and the very dregs of society, the spurious and polluted spawn of the nation.[16]

Josephus continues:

And here I cannot refrain from expressing what my feelings suggest. I am of opinion, that had the Romans deferred the punishment of these wretches, either the earth would have opened and swallowed up the city, or it would have been swept away by a deluge, or have shared the thunderbolts of the land of Sodom. For it produced a race far more ungodly that those who were thus visited. For through desperate madness of these men the whole nation was involved in their ruin.[17]

This generation of Jews in Jesus' time is thoroughly described by Matthew. It was faithless and perverse (17:17), unrepentant, evil and sign-seeking (16:4), ill-tempered and capricious (11:16-19), wicked and very adulterous (16:4), evil speaking, inhumane (23:4, 14), tradition-steeped (15:9), and sinful. It was destined for condemnation (12:42), for it had rejected Christ (Luke 17:25). It was worse than previous generations (12:45). In fact, Jesus promised to heap upon it the blood of prophets from Abel to Zechariah (23:35).

---

[16] Josephus, *Jewish War*, bk. v. c. x. p 5
[17] Josephus, *Jewish Wars* c. xiii. p. 6).

Two verses, Matthew 23:36 and Matthew 24:34, stand as time-frame scriptures that serve as bookends to the Olivet discourse, giving us authority to place the time of the fulfillment of Jesus' prophecy in that first generation. From this authority, we are able to say with confidence that all that Jesus prophesied was to happen before that generation ended. Even though we may want to assume the language of Matthew 24 is speaking of the end of history, these verses bring us back to reality. When Jesus says *all these things* will take place before the disciples' generation is over, He then holds us to contextual interpretation.

> *Now learn this parable from the fig tree: When its branch has already become tender and puts forth leaves, you know that summer is near. So you also, when you see all these things, know that it is near - at the doors! Assuredly, I say to you, this generation will by no means pass away till all these things take place.* (Matt. 24:32-34)

Just as we know when spring is at hand, Jesus told the disciples they could know when these things were to take place. *All these things,* refers namely to a false Christ, earthquakes, wars, abomination of desolation, and so on. This was their warning to flee the city. He was speaking to that generation.

The End of the Age

The Gospels of Mark and Luke, in their record of the Olivet discourse, do not use the Greek word *parousia*, meaning the "presence," and translated in Matthew as "coming." They simply asked when will these things be and what will be the signs. Many Bible scholars wrongly interpret this passage to refer to a future second coming of Christ and the end of the world.

Notice, the term *age* is used rather than *world* when speaking of that which was to come to an end. The Greek word *aion* is used here, meaning "Jewish age, an age, entire completion of a period of time." It is not speaking of the end of the world, but rather of the Mosaic age in which Christ came at the end, as Hebrews says, "but now, once at the **end of the ages,** He has appeared to put away sin by the sacrifice of Himself" (Heb. 9:26). (Emphasis mine.)

The writer of Hebrews tells us, "God . . . has in these last days spoken to us by His Son" (Heb. 1:2).

Peter says that Christ, "was manifest in these last times for you" (1 Peter 1:20).

Paul writing to his contemporaries, the Corinthian church, said, "upon whom the ends of the ages have come" (1 Cor.10:11).

It was *their age* under discussion, not ours. His coming was a *"parousia,"* meaning arrival or presence of a king. He spoke of His coming judgment upon *this* generation. The disciples knew there must be signs that would help them to know when these things would take place. Their interest was not in some future generation, but within their own lifetime. They understood this was their generation and that is why they asked for the sign.

Jesus gave seven signs to His four disciples before He declared *"the* sign." In the next chapter, we will take a look at each of these signs and how they were fulfilled by 70 A.D.

Olivet Discourse
Discussion Questions

1. There are two time-frame scriptures that serve as bookends to the Olivet discourse giving us authority to place the time of the fulfillment of Jesus' prophecy. What are those two scriptures?

2. Jesus said this _____ would not pass away until all these things be fulfilled (Matt. 23:34).

3. In the chapters preceding Matthew 24, Jesus begins to declare judgments upon Israel. What does he say about that generation in the following verses?

    a. Matthew 12:45

    b. Matthew 21:43

    c. Matthew 22:7

    d. Matthew 23:31-36

4. What is the proper translation of the Greek word *aion* in Matthew 24:3?

5. According to Hebrews 9:26, when did Jesus come and die for our sins?

6. Give two New Testament scriptures that show the early church, or that first generation of Christians, lived in the last days.

7. If the end of the age was not the end of the world, then what age was coming to an end?

CHAPTER 5

Signs of the Time

W hen the disciples questioned Jesus about the destruction of the temple, asking when shall these things shall take place, He answered by giving seven signs of the time. These seven signs would lead up to "*the* sign" of the Son of Man in heaven. Let's take a look at the seven signs that Christ gave to that generation.

The First Sign: False Messiahs

For many will come in My name, saying, "I am the Christ," and will mislead many. (Matt. 24:5)

The people were looking for a messiah. They knew the prophets of old had predicted a time when the Messiah would come. Daniel had received revelation concerning the times of his people which pinpointed the time of the Messiah:

And in the days of these kings the God of heaven will set up a kingdom which shall never be destroyed; and the kingdom shall not be left to other people; it shall break in pieces and consume all these kingdoms, and it shall stand forever. (Dan. 2:44)

We see in the Gospel of Luke that the people were in a state of expectation, waiting for the Messiah: "Now as the people were in expectation, and all reasoned in their hearts about John, whether he was the Christ or not" (Luke 3:15). False messiahs rose up early in the church's history during the first century.

We see references to some of these false messiahs in the New Testament. Gamaliel, a Pharisee in the book of Acts, speaks of Theudas who led 400 men to follow him. History tells us a Judas of Galilee also rose up and drew away many after him. Luke records:

> *For some time ago **Theudas** rose up, claiming to be somebody. A number of men, about four hundred, joined him. He was slain, and all who obeyed him were scattered and came to nothing. After this man, Judas of Galilee rose up in the days of the census, and drew away many people after him. He also perished, and all who obeyed him were dispersed* (Acts 5:36, 37).

Ralph Woodrow in *Great Prophecies of the Bible*, points out how Josephus refers to Theudas:

> *According to Josephus, the noted Jewish historian, twelve years after our Saviour's death, a certain impostor named Theudas persuaded a great multitude to follow him to the river Jordan which he claimed would divide for their passage. At the time of Felix (who is mentioned in the Book of Acts), the country of the Jews was filled with impostors who Felix had put to death every day—a statement which indicates that there were 'many' of such in those days.*[18]

Paul was accused of being the Egyptian who raised an insurrection and led 4,000 out into the wilderness as Luke writes: "Are you

---

[18] Ralph Woodrow, *Great Prophecies of the Bible* (Riverside, CA: Ralph Woodrow Evangelistic Association, 1971) 54.

not the Egyptian who some time ago stirred up a rebellion and led the four thousand assassins out into the wilderness?" (Acts 21:38). History tells us, "An Egyptian who 'pretended to be a prophet' gathered 30,000 men, claiming that he would show 'how, at his command, the walls of Jerusalem would fall down.'"[19]

Eusebius of Caesarea, a Roman historian of the third and fourth century, also quoted Justin Martyr in reference to Simon, declaring,

After the Lord was taken up into heaven the demons put forth a number of men who claimed to be gods... for example, Simon, a Samaritan from the village called Goethe, who in Claudius Caesar's time, thanks to the art of the demons who possessed him, worked wonders of magic, and in your imperial city of Rome was regarded as a god... [20]

This is the same Simon is mentioned in Acts: Acts 8:9, 10:

But there was a certain man called Simon, who previously practiced sorcery in the city and astonished the people of Samaria, claiming that he was someone great, to whom they all gave heed, from the least to the greatest, saying, "This man is the great power of God." (Acts 8:9, 10)

Ralph Woodrow, quotes Origen, a church father from the second and third century, of his account:

Origen mentions a certain wonder-worker, Dositheus, who claimed he was the Christ foretold by Moses. Another deceiver in those days was Barchochebas who, according to Jerome, claimed to vomit flames. Bar-jesus is mentioned in Acts 13:6 as a sorcerer and false prophet. These are examples of the deceivers of whom

---

[19] Ralph Woodrow, 54.
[20] Eusebius, *The Nicene and Post-Nicene Fathers,* (Wm. B. Eerdmans Pub. Co., Grand Rapids, MI, Reprint, 1979) 86.

*history says there were 'a great number', and of whom Jesus had
prophesied that there would be many.*[21]

John, the apostle, wrote of these men and others calling them
antichrists. "Little children, it is the last hour; and as you have heard
that the Antichrist is coming, even now many antichrists have come,
by which we know that it is the last hour. They went out from us,
but they were not of us" (1 John 2:18). This first sign was fulfilled
within the generation referred to by Jesus.

The Second Sign: Wars and Rumors of Wars

*You will hear of wars and rumor of wars... Nation will rise
against nation...* (Matt. 24:6)

When Jesus spoke these words, Rome was experiencing what
was called the era of Roman peace. History tells us that for 50 years,
beginning with the reign of Augustus in 17 B.C., Rome experienced
an "age of peace." The words of Jesus were important because they
came during this time of world peace. This peacetime, however, was
fragile, as we see the events of history begin to change after Jesus
prophesied these events.

Josephus, living during the time of the destruction of Jerusalem
in 70 A.D., records the *Jewish wars:*

*Rome had an extension of peace for many years until the
insurrection of Jewish zealots. Out of fear of the Jews rebelling,
Rome tried to squelch the uprisings. In A.D. 40, a disturbance
in Mesopotamia caused 50,000 deaths. In A.D. 49, a tumult
at Jerusalem brought 10-20,000 deaths. At Caesarea, 20,000
Jews were killed and 20,000 died at the hands of the Syrians.
At Scythopolis, more than 13,000 Jews died and thousands*

---

[21] Ralph Woodrow, 54.

were killed in other places. Over 50,000 died in Alexandria, while 10,000 died in a one-hour battle in Damascus. Judea was in revolt against Rome, Awhile the armies of Spain, Gaul and Germany, and Illyricum and Syria converged upon Italy to decide who should succeed to Nero's purple.[22]

Because of the great numbers of wars Josephus states:

I have omitted to give an exact account of them, because they are well known by all, and they are described by a great number of Greek and Roman authors; yet for the sake of connection of matters, and that my history may not be incoherent, I have just touched upon everything briefly.[23]

These troubling times continued to rise leading up to the fall of Jerusalem. Ralph Woodrow writes about these times quoting a first century historian:

Before the fall of Jerusalem, four Emperors came to violent deaths within the space of 18 months. According to the historian Suetonius (who lived during the latter part of the first century and the beginning of the second), Nero "drove a dagger into his throat." Galba was run down by horsemen. A soldier cut off his head and "thrusting his thumb into the mouth," carried the horrid trophy about. Otho "stabbed himself" in the breast. Vitellius was killed by a slow torture and then "dragged by a hook into the Tiber." We can understand that such a fate falling on the Emperors would naturally spread distress and insecurity through the Empire.[24]

---

[22] *The Works of Flavius Josephus.* Vol.1,3
[23] *The Wars of the Jews*, 4:9:2, 688
[24] Ralph Woodrow, *Great Prophecies of the Bible* (Riverside, CA: Ralph Woodrow Evangelistic Association, 1971) 55.

Gary DeMar writes in his book, *Last Days Madness:*

The Annals of Tacitus, covering the period of A.D. 14 to the death of Nero in A.D. 68, describes the tumult of the period with phrases such as "disturbances in Germany," "commotions in Africa," "commotions in Thrace," "insurrections in Gaul," "intrigues among the Parthians," "the war in Britain," and "the war in Armenia."[25]

Wars and rumors of wars were only the beginning of sorrows. Jesus told his disciples, "See that ye be not troubled: for all these things must come to pass, but the END is not yet." The word *end* that is used here is not the same Greek word as in the expression *end of the world*. As Barnes says, the end referred to here is "the end of the Jewish economy; the destruction of Jerusalem."[26]

The Third Sign: Natural Disasters

And there will be famines, pestilence, and earthquakes in various places. (Matt. 24:7)

Jesus warns them of famines, pestilence, and earthquakes. We see where Luke records such events in the Book of Acts that took place during the reign of Claudius, A.D. 41-54. "And there stood up one of them named Agabus, and signified by the Spirit that there should be great death throughout all the world: which came to pass in the days of Claudius Caesar" (Acts 11:28). This famine was so widespread that the church as far away as Corinth participated in relief efforts (1 Corinthians 16:1-5; Romans 15:25-28).

---

[25] Gary DeMar, *Last Days Madness, Obsession of the Modern Church*, (Atlanta, GA: American Vision, 1994) 62.
[26] Woodrow, 55.

Famines affected the entire Roman Empire. DeMar quotes several historians who described this terrible time of distress upon the entire Empire:

Secular historians such as Tacitus (A.D. c.55—c.117), Suetonius, and Josephus mention other famines during the period prior to A.D. 70. In Tacitus we read a description of famine conditions in A.D. 51 in Rome:

"This year witnessed many prodigies [signs or omens] . . . [including] repeated earthquakes . . . Further portents were seen in a shortage of corn, resulting in famine. . . It was established that there was no more than fifteen days' supply of food in the city [of Rome]. Only heaven's special favor and a mild winter prevented catastrophe."[27]

Nothing causes famine like war. The worst of famine for Jerusalem was brought on by the siege of the city by Rome. Josephus records,

Then did the famine widen its progress, and devoured the people by the whole houses and families; the upper rooms were full of women and children that were dying by famine; and the lanes of the city were full of the dead bodies of the aged; the children also and the young men wandered about the marketplaces like shadows, all swelled with the famine, and fell down dead wheresoever their misery seized them.[28]

Josephus wrote of the raging epidemic of diseases that killed thousands in *Babylon.*

[27] Gary DeMar, *Last Days Madness, Obsession of the Modern Church*, (Atlanta, GA: American Vision, 1994) 63-64.
[28] Josephus, *The Wars of the Jews*, 5:12:3, 723.

In A.D. 40, there was a pestilence at Babylon, in which Jews suffered.[29] *"In A.D. 66, there was much death at Rome on account of a pestilence."*[30]

During this period, Jesus said there would be great earthquakes. A great earthquake was recorded in Acts 16:26. It was so mighty that even the foundations of the prison shook. Ralph Woodrow writes concerning this same period and quotes Tacitus, "frequent earthquakes occurred, by which many houses were thrown down" and that "twelve populous cities of Asia fell in ruins from an earthquake."[31] Speaking of these cities destroyed, Marcellus Kik, in his book, *An Eschatology of Victory*, explains, "There were earthquakes in Crete, Smyrna, Miletus, Chios, Samos, Laodicea, Hierapolis, Colosse, Campania, Rome, and Judea. It is interesting to note that the city of Pompeii was much damaged by an earthquake occurring on February 5, 63 A.D."[32]

Jesus was not talking about earthquakes in our future, but during the days leading up to the destruction of Jerusalem. That is why this was such a sign to those of that generation. The number of earthquakes during this period was overwhelming. Josephus describes one earthquake of such magnitude, "that the constitution of the universe was confounded for the destruction of men."[33]

The Book of Revelation was written to the seven churches of Asia. Originally, the apostle Paul established nine churches in that area, but only seven were addressed in Revelation. The reason for this is that the cities of Colosse, Hierapolis, and Laodicea, were all

---

[29] Josephus, *Antiquities*, XVIII.IX.8, 395.

[30] Tacitus, *The Histories*, 4 vols, trans, Clifford H. Moore, (Cambridge, MA: Harvard University, 1962) 16.13, 5-7.

[31] Woodrow, 56.

[32] Marcellus J. Kik, *An Eschatology of Victory*, (Phillipsburg, NJ: Presbyterian and Reformed, 1971) 93.

[33] Josephus, *Antiquities*, IV., 4.

destroyed by an earthquake around AD 61. Laodicea was rebuilt soon afterwards, but the other two cities were not. This left only seven churches in Asia during the five years just prior to the beginning of the Roman/Jewish war which took place at the end of the 40-year generation of which Jesus spoke.

The Fourth Sign: Persecution and Tribulation

Then they will deliver you up to tribulation and kill you, ...for My name's sake. (Matt. 24:9)

Beginning in the early days of the apostles in the book of Acts we see many of these persecutions. The apostles were arrested by authorities in Acts 4 through 8. Stephen was the first to be killed, in Acts 7, but the persecutions grew against the Christians both by the Jews and Romans. It was mentioned in Acts 8, that "great persecution" broke out against the church and they were scattered throughout Judea and Samaria.

James the brother of John was cut down by a sword.

Now about that time Herod the king stretched out his hand to harass some from the church. Then he killed James the brother of John with the sword. And because he saw that it pleased the Jews, he proceeded further to seize Peter also. Now it was during the Days of Unleavened Bread. (Acts 12:1-3)

Paul writes concerning his own persecutions:

From the Jews five times I received forty stripes minus one. Three times I was beaten with rods; once I was stoned; three times I was shipwrecked; a night and a day I have been in the deep; in journeys often, in perils of waters, in perils of robbers, in perils of my own countrymen, in perils of the Gentiles, in perils in the city, in perils in the wilderness, in perils in the sea, in

perils among false brethren; in weariness and toil, in sleepless-
ness often, in hunger and thirst, in fastings often, in cold and
nakedness. (2 Cor. 11:24-27)

All the apostles, except John, were martyred by 70 A.D. Persecutions and tribulations reached their pinnacle under Nero before
his death in 68 A.D. Paul lost his life to the persecution of Nero. As
Tertullian wrote, "There was war against the very name of Christ."[34]
Jesus warned His disciples:

Look, I am sending you out as sheep among wolves. So be as
shrewd as snakes and harmless as doves. But beware! For you
will be handed over to the courts and will be flogged with whips
in the synagogues. You will stand trial before governors and kings
because you are my followers. But this will be your opportunity
to tell the rulers and other unbelievers about me. When you are
arrested, don't worry about how to respond or what to say. God
will give you the right words at the right time. For it is not
you who will be speaking—it will be the Spirit of your Father
speaking through you.

A brother will betray his brother to death, a father will betray
his own child, and children will rebel against their parents and
cause them to be killed. And all nations will hate you because
you are my followers. But everyone who endures to the end will
be saved. When you are persecuted in one town, flee to the next.
I tell you the truth, the Son of Man will return before you have
reached all the towns of Israel. (Matt. 10:16-23)

This warning was fulfilled by the persecution that came to the
disciples during their lifetime, before the destruction of Jerusalem.
Jesus referenced His coming in judgment by saying they would not

---

[34] DeMar, 83.

have reached all the towns of Israel before He would return. He was not talking about the second coming, as He was speaking to His own disciples living in His day. To misunderstand this and say that Jesus was speaking of His second coming, would be to do what they did in His day when He spoke to Peter of John, "If I want him to remain alive until I return, what is that to you? You must follow me. Because of this, the rumor spread among the believers that this disciple would not die. But Jesus did not say that he would not die; he only said, If I want him to remain alive until I return, what is that to you?" (John 21:22, 23)

The Fifth Sign: A Great Falling Away or Apostasy

And then many will be offended, will betray one another, and will hate one another. Then many false prophets will rise up and deceive many. And because lawlessness will abound, the love of many will grow cold. (Matt. 24:10-12)

As leaders were killed and deceptions came, many grew cold in their walk with Christ. Paul warns the church constantly of deceivers, wolves, and false apostles, who would turn many from the faith. Paul called the elders together in Ephesus and warned them saying,

"For I know this, that after my departure savage wolves will come in among you, not sparing the flock. Also from among yourselves men will rise up, speaking perverse things, to draw away the disciples after themselves." (Acts 20:29, 30)

He spoke of these perilous times in those "last days" before the destruction of Jerusalem. When Paul wrote to Timothy he was warning him of the same apostasy that Jesus spoke of in that generation. Many today are looking for a future falling away, but Jesus spoke of that generation. Paul wrote of those days:

But know this, that in the last days perilous times will come: For men will be lovers of themselves, lovers of money, boasters, proud, blasphemers, disobedient to parents, unthankful, unholy, unloving, unforgiving, slanderers, without self- control, brutal, despisers of good, traitors, headstrong, haughty, lovers of pleasure rather than lovers of God, having a form of godliness but denying its power. And from such people turn! (2 Tim. 3:1-9)

Now the Spirit expressly says that in latter times some will depart from the faith, giving heed to deceiving spirits and doctrines of demons. (1 Tim. 4:1)

The apostle Peter also warns of an apostasy by declaring false teachers and prophets among believers.

But there were also false prophets among the people, even as there will be false teachers among you, who will secretly bring in destructive heresies, even denying the Lord who bought them, and bring on themselves swift destruction. (2 Pet. 2:1)

Once again, Jesus' prophetic warnings were fulfilled in the generation before the destruction of Jerusalem in AD 70.

The Sixth Sign: Gospel of The Kingdom Will Be Preached in The Whole World

And this gospel of the kingdom will be preached in all the world as a witness to all the nations, and then the end will come. (Matt. 24:14)

As one of the signs, Jesus said the gospel of the kingdom would be preached to the whole world. Remember, Jesus said all these things would take place before that generation was over. God gave the Jews an entire generation to repent and see Him as the Messiah. For 40 years, the gospel went forth to the entire known Roman Empire.

The Greek word for world is *oikoumene,* meaning the inhabited world; specifically, the Roman empire. The gospel of the kingdom went out into all the known world. It was preached to every creature under heaven. When Paul was writing in A.D. 64, he declares, "the gospel, which you heard, which was preached to every creature under heaven..." (Col. 1:23)

He again mentions the *world* in verse 6: "*In the same way, the gospel is bearing fruit and growing throughout the whole world--just as it has been doing among you since the day you heard it and truly understood God's grace"* (Col. 1:6).

Ralph Woodrow makes clear how the growth of the gospel message spread during the time of Nero, fulfilling what Jesus said.

> *By the time of Nero, the Christians had grown so numerous that they aroused the jealousy of the government. The story of the great fire in Rome in 64 A.D.—for which the Christians were falsely blamed—is well known.*

He continues citing others to explain how the gospel had spread to Europe,

> *Concerning even far away England, Newton says: 'There is absolute certainty that Christianity was planted in this country in the days of the apostles, before the destruction of Jerusalem.' Eusebius and also Theodoret inform us that the apostles preached the gospel in all the world and some of them passed beyond the ocean to the Britannic isles.*[35]

Paul opens his epistle to the Romans by saying:

"Your faith is spoken of throughout the **whole world."** (Rom 1:8)

---

[35] Woodrow, 60.

"Yes indeed: their sound has gone out **to all the earth**, and their **words to the ends of the world.**" *(*Rom 10:18)

And again he declares concerning the gospel, *it has been made manifest, . . . to all nations . . .*" (Rom. 16:25, 26) (Emphasis mine.)

The gospel preached as a witness was important before judgment came. God always allows opportunity for repentance. Here, even as the children of Israel were given forty years to repent in the wilderness, Christ declares the gospel would be preached to the known world before the end of that age. Then judgment would come.

The Seventh Sign: Abomination of Desolation

So when you see standing in the holy place "the abomination that causes desolation," spoken of through the prophet Daniel— let the reader understand— then let those who are in Judea flee to the mountains. (Matt. 24:16, 17)

The Gospel of Matthew refers to the abomination of desolation in reference to the prophet Daniel (Dan. 9:27; 11:31; 12:11). Matthew was writing to a Jewish audience and he knew they were well aware of those terms. Luke refers to this same event but does not use Daniel's reference. Rather he explains the interpretation while writing to Gentiles. Luke tells us the abomination of desolation was the Roman armies coming to destroy the city and the temple. These were also the words of Jesus that Luke quoted, "But when you see Jerusalem surrounded by armies, then, know that its desolation is near" (Luke 21:20).

The abomination of desolation is explained further in the *Commentary on the Gospel of Mark:*

Josephus found the fulfillment of Daniel in the events of A.D. 66-70 (Antiquities X. xi. 7; In the same manner Daniel also wrote about the empire of the Romans and that Jerusalem would be taken and the Temple laid waste'). He refers to an ancient prophecy concerning the desecration of the Temple by Jewish hands and found its fulfillment in whole series of villainous acts committed by the Zealots in the Temple precincts from the period November, A.D. 67 to the spring of 68.[36]

The followers of Jesus listened and understood Jesus' prophecy because when they saw Jerusalem surrounded by the Roman armies, they departed and fled to the mountains of Judea. Woodrow quotes Josephus, and tells us,

Cestius and his armies were being very successful in their battle against Jerusalem. So much so, in fact, that the Jews were ready to give up and shortly would have opened their gates in surrender—thus saving the city and temple. But prophecy had it that these things would be destroyed! When Cestius would have almost taken the city, suddenly—as Josephus says, "without any reason in the world"— he withdrew his troops and departed! This filled the Jews with courage and they pursued the retreating army inflicting on it a major disaster.[37]

Truly the disciples believed Jesus' words and obeyed. We have more than one source confirming that no Christian lost their lives in the destruction of Jerusalem, because they did, in fact, escape.

Thomas Newton, an English Anglican theologian, wrote concerning the Roman armies surrounding Jerusalem before its destruction:

---

36 William L. Lande, *Commentary on the Gospel of Mark* (Grand Rapids, MI: Eerdmans, 1974), 468-69.
37 Woodrow, 64.

We learn from ecclesiastical histories, that at this juncture all who believe in Christ departed Jerusalem, and removed to Pella and other places beyond the river Jordan; so that they all marvelously escaped the general shipwreck of their countrymen; and we do not read anywhere that so much as one of them perished in the destruction of Jerusalem."[38]

All seven signs were fulfilled before the generation living during the time of Christ passed away. In less than forty years, the length of a generation, all that Jesus prophesied took place before the destruction of Jerusalem, AD 70.

---

[38] Newton, *Dissertations on the Prophecies*, 389; also see Eusebius, *Ecclesiastical History*, Bk 3, chapter 5; Edersheim, *Life and Times of Jesus the Messiah*, 448.

Signs of the Time
Discussion Questions

1. Name the seven signs that Jesus gave to His disciples.

    a.

    b.

    c.

    d.

    e.

    f.

    g.

2. Who was the false Christ that lead four hundred to follow him?

3. Historically Rome had known an _____ of peace for fifty years before Jesus prophesied wars.

4. What prophet in the book of Acts foretold of the famine coming to the known world even as Jesus did?

5. How many of the apostles were martyred before 70 A.D.?

6. What two verses tell us that the gospel of the kingdom was preached in all the world during Paul's day?

7. Jesus interprets the Roman _____ as being the fulfillment of desolation spoken of by the prophet Daniel.

CHAPTER 6

The Great Tribulation

For then there will be great tribulation, such as has not been since the beginning of the world until this time, no, nor ever shall be. (Matt. 24:21)

Clear, Distinct Warnings

Jesus' prophecy gave a warning to the Christians to flee to the mountains of Judea when they saw the armies surrounding Jerusalem. Christians, both in Jerusalem and in the countryside of Judea, were told, "Let those who are in the midst of her depart, and let not those who are in the country enter her. For these are the days of vengeance, that all things which are written may be fulfilled" (Luke 21:21, 22).

When Jesus spoke of the *"days of vengeance"* that were to come upon all of Israel, He spoke of the judgments that would come to pass upon that generation. His urgency was communicated by declaring, "Let him who is on the housetop not come down to take anything out of his house, and let him in the field not go back to get his clothes" (Matt 24:17, 18).

Jesus said how dreadful it would be for pregnant mothers and for those who were nursing babies because the trip to the mountains of Judea would be difficult. The Master told them to pray for the opportunity to leave Jerusalem when it was not winter or the Sabbath. The reason these warnings were so important was that they pointed out the fact that this was a real army coming to surround Jerusalem, and the fulfillment of the abomination spoken of by the prophet Daniel. The opportunity to escape was to be so short, the urgency was given to leave immediately when they saw the armies. They must have believed Jesus' prophecies. *Adam Clark's Commentary* tells us that when Jerusalem was surrounded by Cestius Gallus, that he withdrew allowing Christians to flee.[39] Quoting Josephus, Woodrow explains, though no Christians lost their life, more than one million Jews were killed and nearly one hundred thousand were led into captivity in fulfillment of Luke 21:24.[40]

The contextual authority of the Olivet discourse does not allow us to place these warnings into the future, referring to the second coming of Christ. This can only refer to the need to escape to the mountains because of the approaching armies. The Talmud law limited travel on the Sabbath, so the Christians would not have been allowed to escape on a Sabbath. Furthermore, why would a nursing mother be concerned at the second coming of Christ? There is no reason to give such a warning concerning the second coming of Jesus, but there are logical and adequate reasons to warn nursing mothers of the hardships encountered in traveling in those days to a place of refuge. It was significant that their flight not be in the winter months for obvious reasons of the cold. The first century Christians must have obeyed Jesus and prayed, because their flight

---

[39] *Clarke's Commentary*, Vol 1, Matthew-Acts, 228.
[40] Woodrow, 75.

was not on the Sabbath nor in winter, but in the fall of A.D. 66, according to Josephus. Jesus was precise in His warnings because He was speaking to that particular generation of people.

As we have seen, history tells us that Cestius Gallus surrounded the city of Jerusalem with Roman armies. Bray gives us the details when Cestius entered Jerusalem:

> *October 15-22, A.D. 66. The 'war' group (the Zealots) were in control of the city by this time. The Roman army pitched close to Jerusalem on Mount Scopus. On November 17 Cestius led his troops into Jerusalem. They soon lost this battle against the Jews and withdrew and fled... The Christians took advantage of this 'lull' in the war, and escaped from the city and fled to Pella.*[41]

> *The next year, Nero sent Vespasian to Judea to stop the rebellion. His commission from Nero was in A.D. 67, and the declaration of war against Judea occurred in the early part of February of that year. (It was three years and six months later, on August 10, A.D. 70, that Jerusalem was destroyed. This is the 42 months during which the holy city was to be given to the Gentiles to tread under foot, according to Revelation 11:2.*[42]

The Significance of Apostate Israel

Jesus wanted His disciples to be warned of the coming judgment upon natural Israel. Such a destruction could not be matched with any previous judgment or any following. This would be the tribulation of all tribulations. Today we hardly understand the significance of apostate Israel. We see these events through the eyes of 2000 years of Christianity. What we must understand, is that Jerusalem

---

[41] John Bray, *Matthew 24 Fulfilled*, (Lakeland, FL: John L Bray Ministries Inc, 1996) 68.
[42] Bray, 68-69.

represented the headquarters of the earth for the Jewish people. God had established His house, the temple, and required that every male come to worship three times a year. This was the center of God's relationship with man in the earth. Now Jesus is speaking of the destruction of this same temple. The impact of such an event would be like none other. That is why He uses the words, "such has not been since the beginning of the world until this time, no, nor ever shall be." Nothing could be more dramatic than for God to change the way He dwelt with man. When the scriptures tell us in John 1:14, that Jesus came and "dwelt among us," He became our temple. After the death, burial, and resurrection, He ascended into Heaven and sent the Holy Spirit to dwell among the Christians, and they then became the "temple of God." This was a major change. It was the fulfillment of all that God had purposed before time began.

This coming judgment was always on Jesus' mind. As he was being led away to be crucified, Jesus warned of this destruction:

> ...*Daughters of Jerusalem, do not weep for Me, but weep for yourselves and for your children. For indeed the days are coming in which they will say, "Blessed are the barren, the wombs that never bore, and the breasts which never nursed!" Then they will say to the mountains, "Fall on us!" and to the hills, "Cover us!"* (Luke 23:28-30)

He knew that before that generation was over, Jerusalem would be destroyed and the kingdom taken from them and given to another, just as was said, "this generation will by no means pass away till all these things are fulfilled" (Matt. 24:34).

The Change of Order

The events that took place during the siege of Jerusalem, from the fall of A.D. 66 until the destruction in A.D. 70, show a tremendous tribulation and a change of order. Jesus told them that the *abomination of desolation* would be the Gentile armies surrounding Jerusalem leading to its destruction. Daniel prophesied of the same coming armies who would destroy Jerusalem and the Temple, and finish the days of his people:

> *The people of the prince who is to come will destroy the city and the sanctuary. And its end will come with a flood; even to the end there will be war; desolations are determined . . . And on the wing of abominations will come one who makes desolate, even until a complete destruction, one that is decreed, is poured out upon the desolate.* (Dan. 9:26, 27)

Before the end of that generation, Jerusalem was surrounded by heathen armies. The Idumeans, or Edomites, the longtime enemies of Israel, surrounded and attacked Jerusalem. According to Josephus:

> *One evening in A.D. 68, the Edomites surrounded the holy city with 20,000 soldiers. As they lay outside the wall, according to Josephus, there broke out a prodigious storm in the night, with the utmost violence, and very strong winds, with the largest showers of rain, with continual lightnings, terrible thunderings, and amazing concussions and bellowings of the earth that was in an earthquake. These things were a manifest indication that some destruction was coming upon men, when the system of the world was put into this disorder; and anyone would guess that these wonders foreshowed some grand calamities that were coming.*

> *This was the last opportunity to escape from the doomed city of Jerusalem. Anyone who wished to flee had to do so immediately, without delay. The Edomites broke into the city and went directly to the Temple, where they slaughtered 8,500 people by slitting their throats. As the Temple overflowed with blood, the*

Edomites rushed, plundering houses and murdering everyone they met, including the high priest. According to the historian Josephus, this event marked "the beginning of the destruction of the city... from this very day may be dated the overthrow of her wall and the ruin of her affairs."[43]

Josephus has left us an eyewitness record of much of the horror of those years, especially of the final days in Jerusalem.

It was a time when "the daytime was spent in the shedding of blood, and the night in fear" when it was "common to see cities filled with dead bodies;" when Jews panicked and began indiscriminately killing each other in order to prevent them from receiving worse treatment from the Romans; when, in the midst of terrible famine, mothers killed, roasted, and ate their own children (cf. Deuteronomy 28:53); when the whole land "was all over filled with fire and blood;" when the lakes and seas turned red, dead bodies floating everywhere, littering the shores, bloating in the sun, rotting and splitting apart; when the Roman soldiers captured people attempting to escape, then crucified them—at the rate of 500 per day.[44]

The city of Jerusalem came under siege after this event by the Edomites. During this long period of siege, excruciating famine forced judgment upon Israel as recorded in the curses of Deuteronomy 28, "You shall eat the fruit of your own body, the flesh of your sons and daughters whom the Lord your God has given you, in the siege and desperate straits in which your enemy shall distress you" (Deut. 28:53).

---

[43] David Chilton, *Paradise Restored* (Tyler, TX: Reconstruction Press, 1985) 92.
[44] David Chilton, *The Great Tribulation* (Forth Worth, TX: Dominion Press) 12-14.

Josephus once again recorded the fulfillment of scripture during the siege of Jerusalem under Rome.

Then did the famine widen its progress, and devoured the people by whole houses and families; the upper rooms were full of women and children that were dying by famine; and the lanes of the city were full of the dead bodies of the aged; the children also and the young men wandered about the marketplaces like shadows, all swelled with the famine, and fell down dead wheresoever their misery seized them.

In the meantime, countless thousands of Jews died of hunger. In every house where there was the least morsel of food, relatives fought over it. Gaping with hunger, the outlaws prowled around like mad dogs, gnawing at anything: belts, shoes, and even the leather from their shields. Others devoured wisps of hay, and then there was the incredible horror of Mary of Bethezuba.

Distinguished in family and fortune, Mary had fled to Jerusalem from Perea, but her property had been plundered by the tyrants during the siege, and her food by the daily raids of their followers. Maddened by hunger, she seized the infant at her breast and said, "Poor baby, why should I preserve you for war, famine, and rebellion? Come, be my food- vengeance against the rebels, and the climax of Jewish tragedy for the world." With that, she killed her infant son, roasted his body, and devoured half of it, hiding the remainder.

Instantly the rebels arrived, sniffing the unholy smell and threatening her with death if she did not produce what she had prepared. She had reserved a fine portion for them too, she replied, uncovering the remnants of her baby. They stood paralyzed with horror. "This is my child and my action," she said. "Help your-selves; for I've had my share. Don't be weaker than a woman or more compassionate than a mother! But if you're squeamish and disapprove of my sacrifice, then leave the rest for me."

They left trembling, and the whole city rocked with this abom-ination, while the Romans were horrified, and Caesar declared himself innocent of this crime in the sight of God. He swore, however, to bury this atrocity of infant cannibalism beneath the ruins of the country.[45]

John Bray quotes from Josephus to show the significance of the days of assault on the city.

As the siege continued the miseries of the Jews grew worse, and finally the Romans made an assault on the tower of Antonia. This assault was made on July 17, A.D. 70. . . The daily sacrifice ceased July 17th, because the hands were all needed for defense. . . From the time that Vespasian declared war on Judea (Spring of A.D. 67) until cessation of sacrifices in the Temple (July 17, A.D. 70), was approximately 3 1/2 years.[46]

Burning of Jerusalem

When Titus and the Roman armies finally entered the temple in Jerusalem, it was August 9. The next day, August 10, was the day that the first temple was destroyed by Babylon 600 years prior.[47] Josephus tell us Titus wanted to save the temple, "so magnificent a work as the temple ought to be spared because it would always be an ornament to the empire." However, the soldiers rushed in with such

---

[45] *Josephus, The Essential Writings, New Translation and Edited by Paul L. Maier* (Grand Rapids, MI: Kregel Publications, 1998) 358-359.
[46] Bray, 74.
[47] Bray, 76

rage, pretending not to hear his orders, and set flames to the temple and began a slaughter.

> *When the temple was in flames, the victors stole everything they could lay their hands on, and slaughtered all who were caught. No pity was shown to age or rank, old men or children, the laity or priest—all were massacred. As flames roared up, and since the temple stood on a hill, it seemed as if the whole city were ablaze. The noise was deafening, with war cries of the legions, howls of the rebels surrounded by fire and sword, and the shrieks of the people. The ground was hidden by corpses, and the soldiers had to climb over heaps of bodies in pursuit of the fugitives.*[48]

Jesus prophesied in Luke 21:11, *There shall be terrors and great portents (signs) from heaven* [*New Testament in Modern English*].

Josephus recorded such events.

> *Before the siege, however, portents had appeared, foretelling the impending devastation, but the Jews had disregarded these warnings of God. A star resembling a sword hung over the city, and also a comet which lasted a year. And just before the revolt, when the people were coming together for the feast of the Unleavened Bread, a bright light shone around the altar during the night and brightened the sanctuary for half an hour. The people thought this a good omen, but the sacred scribes told them the contrary. A cow gave birth to a lamb in the temple court, and the eastern gate of the inner court, which was fastened with iron bars and so heavy that it took twenty men to move it, flew open on its own during the night.*[49]

---

[48] *Josephus*, 361.
[49] *Josephus*, 362.

When the temple was under attack, the rebel Jews fled into the city of Jerusalem. This fulfilled the desolation spoken by the prophet Daniel. "The Roman armies pitched their standards inside the temple court and offered sacrifice, acclaiming Titus as imperator."[50]

Finding little resistance, the Romans poured, "into the streets [of the upper city]. They massacred everyone they found, burning the houses with all who had taken shelter in them. So great was the slaughter that in many places the flames were put out by the streams of blood."[51]

History tells us the total number of Jewish prisoners taken during the war was estimated at 97,000 and those who died during the siege 1,100,000.[52] The judgment of God had truly come upon those of that generation for all the righteous blood shed from Abel to Zacharias.

[50] *Josephus,* 363.
[51] *Josephus,* 365.
[52] John Bray, *Matthew 24 Fulfilled,* (Lakeland, FL: John L Bray Ministries Inc, 1996) 81-82.

Great Tribulation
Discussion Questions

1. Where did Jesus tell those who were from Judea to flee?

2. Why did Jesus tell the disciples that anyone who was on top of their house to not take the time to go in and get anything, and why did He tell those who would be in the field to not go back to the house?

3. What did the temple and Jerusalem represent to the nation of Israel?

4. Why did Jesus warn the daughters of Jerusalem to not weep for him but to weep for themselves?

5. Why do you think Jesus told the disciples to pray that it would not be winter when they had to flee to the mountains?

6. According to Jesus (Luke 21:20-22), what sign was going to be given to the disciples or Christians that they were to flee to the mountains?

7. According to the Jewish historian Josephus, how many Jewish people lost their lives in the siege and destruction of Jerusalem?

CHAPTER 7

The Powers Shall be Shaken

*For anyone who tells you, "There he is, out in the desert," do
not go out; or, "Here he is, in the inner rooms; do not believe it.
For as lightning that comes from the east is visible even in the
west, so will be the coming of the Son of Man. Wherever there is
a carcass, there the vultures will gather. "Immediately after the
distress of those days " 'the sun will be darkened, and the moon
will not give its light; the stars will fall from the sky, and the
heavenly bodies will be shaken.'"* (Matt. 24:26-29)

No Small Thing

Speaking in His day, Jesus warned His disciples that many false
Christs were coming and they were not to be deceived to go out
looking for them. As He gave signs leading up to His coming in
judgment, He let them know it would be no small thing, and would
not be hidden. *John Gill's Commentary* explains:

> *So shall the coming of the son of man be, which must be under-
> stood not of his last coming to judgment, though that will be
> sudden, visible, and universal. . .but of his coming in his wrath*

and vengeance to destroy that people, their nation, city, and temple: so that after this to look for the Messiah in a desert, or secret chamber, must argue great stupidity and blindness; when his coming was as sudden, visible, powerful, and general, to the destruction of that nation, as the lightning that comes from the east, and, in a moment, shines to the west.[53]

Jesus uses the words, "Wherever there is a carcass, there the vultures will gather." He is pointing out the focus of His prophetic word is still on Jerusalem, which now is a dead body or a carcass. Jesus had just told them their house was left desolate or uninhabited. God no longer dwelt there. It was once His house, now it is *their* house and is empty. "The vultures will gather," is in reference to the Gentile armies of Rome that would surround the city after the siege and bring an end to the power of the city. Some translations interpret the word "vultures" as "eagles." If that is the case, then it more clearly points to the Roman armies of which had an ensign of an eagle.[54]

What did Jesus mean that His coming would be like lightning from east and visible from the west? Gary DeMar, in his book *Is Jesus Coming Soon?* explains:

Jesus told His people that He would come "just as lightning comes from the east," that is, quickly and without warning. In the Bible, lightning often signifies the presence of the Lord or His coming in judgment (Ex. 19:16; 20:18; Job 36:30; Ezek. 21:15, 28; Zech. 9:14). God was not physically present during any of these Old Testament comings, but His presence was obvious. Deuteronomy 33:2 says, "The Lord came from Sinai, and dawned on them from Seir; He shone forth from Mount Paran, and He came from the midst of ten thousand holy ones; at His

---

[53] *John Gill's Exposition of the Bible*, Matthew 24:27
[54] Bray, 116.

right hand there was flashing lightning for them." Was God physically present during these times? No. Did He really come? Most certainly![55]

End of The Mosaic Age

Many people see Matthew 24, in reference to the second coming of Christ. However, there is no mention of the resurrection nor the end of history. What was coming to an end was the Mosaic age. The word for *coming* in Matthew 24, is "Parousia," meaning *presence.* Jesus was talking about the coming judgment against the apostate Israel who had not only rejected the Messiah, but had also ignored His reign for a generation. They had continued on as if God's Son, the Messiah, had never come to this earth. Jesus told them that upon them would come all the righteous blood that had been shed on the earth. This is the "finishing of the transgression" spoken about in Daniel 9:24.

The tribulation of "those days" was to the Jewish people undergoing the siege of the Roman armies and the atrocities of God's judgments upon them. Jesus warns, "Immediately after the tribulation of those days shall the sun be darkened and the moon shall not give her light, and the stars shall fall from heaven, and the powers of the heavens shall be shaken" (Matt. 24:29). The terms we often associate with the end of the world are used in this passage. Jesus uses apocalyptic language. Powers of the heavens shaken, the sun being darkened, the moon not giving light, and the stars falling from heaven, all sound like the end of the world.

Adam Clarke's Commentary explains verse twenty-nine,

Lord is not speaking of any distant event, but of something immediately consequent on calamities already predicted: and

---

[55] Gary DeMar, *Is Jesus Coming Soon?* (Power Spring, GA: American Vision Inc., 2006, first edition, 1999), 50.

that must be the destruction of Jerusalem. "The Jewish heaven shall perish, and the sun and moon of its glory and happiness shall be darkened—brought to nothing.[56]

Let the Bible Interpret the Bible

Remember, we must always let the Bible interpret the Bible, and we must also keep our interpretation in the context of the scripture and not our presuppositions. Where else in the scriptures do we see such language and what happened then? In Isaiah 13, the prophet is given to prophesy against Babylon. Babylon was the great nation represented by the golden head of the image that King Nebuchadnezzar saw in his dream that Daniel interpreted to mean Babylon. Daniel said there would be another nation coming after it that would take the powers from Babylon. That nation would be Medo-Persia. According to verse 17, the prophecy of Isaiah 13 speaks of this event. Notice in verse 10, it uses the same apocalyptic language as in Matthew 24 in describing the end of Babylon by the Medes: "The stars of heaven and their constellations will not show their light. The rising sun will be darkened and the moon will not give its light" (Is. 13:10). In other words, it was over for Babylon. There was a power change. It was a dark day in Babylon. The stars, sun, and moon did not literally cease to give light, but rather biblical imagery is used here to describe a "dark day" in the history of this nation.

We also see this same language used when Babylon took over Egypt. The prophet Ezekiel declared God's warning:

When I snuff you out, I will cover the heavens and darken their stars; I will cover the sun with a cloud, and the moon will not give its light. All the shining lights in the heavens I will

---

[56] *Adam Clarke's Commentary*, Matthew 24:29.

darken over you; I will bring darkness over your land, declares the Sovereign Lord. (Ez. 32:7, 8)

What is God saying here in Ezekiel? God is saying the same thing Jesus is saying to Israel in Matthew 24, and the same thing Isaiah prophesied to Babylon. Their day was over. Their lights were going out. The day of God's judgment had come to their nation. It was their *day of the Lord.*

Once again, the prophet Isaiah is told to prophesy against Edom and Bozrah. God says, "All the stars of the heavens will be dissolved and the sky rolled up like a scroll; all the starry host will fall like withered leaves from the vine, like shriveled figs from the fig tree" (Isa. 34:4). This terminology is the same that is spoken against apostate Israel in Amos 8:9 in reference to the same time period in which Jesus prophesies in Matthew 24, "In that day, declares the Lord, I will make the sun go down at noon and darken the earth in broad daylight" (Amos 8:9).

We see the Old Testament prophet, Jeremiah, also used the same kind of language that Jesus chose in Matthew 24. When Jeremiah spoke of the first destruction of Jerusalem and the temple by the Chaldeans he uses the same biblical language.

> *I beheld the earth, and indeed it was without form, and void; and the heavens, they had no light. I beheld the mountains, and indeed they trembled, and all the hills moved back and forth . . . The whole land shall be desolate; yet I will not make a full end. For this shall the earth mourn, and the heavens above be black . . .* (Jer. 4:23-28)

Jeremiah speaks of temporal judgment by the Babylonians in 586 B.C. and uses natural phenomena as a way to communicate the judgment of God. The prophet says that God will not make a full end under Babylon, because the full end would come later in the destruction of Jerusalem under Rome as Jesus prophesied.

In each of the above passages, the contextual authority makes clear that symbolism and pictorial language are being used to describe the end of one government and the beginning of another. The stars, sun, and moon are often seen in the scriptures as referring to authority. One example was in the dream of Joseph where the sun, moon, and stars bowed down to him. Israel is seen in Revelation 12, as the woman clothed with the sun, the moon, and the stars from which Christ the Son was to come.

The book of Revelation is a detailed look at the same subject of Matthew 24. Matthew 24, is often called the "little apocalypse." We see the identical language used in Revelation in reference to the same event mentioned in Matthew 24:29.

And the stars of heaven fell to the earth, as a fig tree drops its late figs when it is shaken by a mighty wind. Then the sky receded as a scroll when it is rolled up, and every mountain and island was moved out of its place. And the kings of the earth, the great men, the rich men, the commanders, the mighty men, every slave and every free man, hid themselves in the caves and in the rocks of the mountains, and said to the mountains and rocks, "Fall on us and hide us from the face of Him who sits on the throne and from the wrath of the Lamb!" (Rev. 6:13-16)

Woodrow explains how:

God repeatedly warned his people in the Old Testament that if they did not repent, disaster and destruction would fall upon them. It would be a day of 'darkness, and not light ... even very dark, and no brightness in it' (Amos 5:18-20). 'The end is coming upon my people Israel ... I will cause the SUN to go down at noon, and I will DARKEN the earth in the clear day' (Amos 8:2, 9). They would be scattered in a 'cloudy and DARK day" (Ezekiel 34:12).[57]

The powers of heaven were about to be shaken. The government of Moses was being brought to an end. Even though Jesus had already officially changed the priesthood and government from Moses to Christ, the Jews had not recognized it, nor had they ceased their operations. The nation of Israel, who was to bring forth the Messiah had, in fact, rejected Him in the greatest way. The writer of Hebrews addresses the same problem as a contemporary to the day just before the destruction of Jerusalem:

> See to it that you do not refuse him who speaks. If they did not escape when they refused him who warned us from heaven, how much less will we, if we turn away from him who warns us from heaven? At that time his voice shook the earth, but now he has promised, "Once more I will shake not only the earth but also the heavens." Now this, "Yet once more," indicates the removal of those things that are being shaken, as of things that are made, that the things which cannot be shaken may remain."
> (Heb. 12:25-27)

The things that are being removed are the elements of the old covenant order under Moses that had been kept as a result of the temple still standing. Only the kingdom of God was to remain after the destruction of the temple and Jerusalem—and this kingdom cannot be shaken. Daniel the prophet, tells of this day when he declares, "In the time of those kings, the God of heaven will set up a kingdom that will never be destroyed, nor will it be left to another people" (Dan. 2:44).

---

[57] Woodrow, 82.

The writer of Hebrews specifically says the obsolete aspects of the old covenant were in the process of vanishing away while he was writing in the first century, prior to the fall of Jerusalem in A.D. 70. Hebrews says, "By calling this covenant 'new,' he has made the first one obsolete; and what is obsolete and aging will soon disappear" (Heb. 8:13).

The powers that were to be shaken were none other than the seat of Moses with the nation of Israel. The kingdom would be removed from them and given to Israel (the church), under the Lordship of the Messiah. This new nation made up of both Jews and Gentiles would bring forth fruit of it and they are called the "holy nation" (1 Peter 2:9).

The Powers Shall be Shaken
Discussion Questions

1. According to Isaiah 13, when the powers of heaven where shaken and the stars fell from heaven, one nation was losing its power and another was taking over. What nation was having its lights put out?

2. When Babylon took over Egypt (Ezek. 32:7-8), what similar language to Matthew 24:29 was used to describe this event?

3. When the Babylonians destroyed Jerusalem the first time, Jeremiah predicted certain things would take place. What were these events?

4. What do stars, sun, and moon often represent?

5. Hebrews tells of powers to be shaken. What were the powers that were to be shaken of which Jesus spoke in Matthew 24?

CHAPTER 8

The Sign of the Kingdom

The Son of Man is in Heaven

The destruction of Jerusalem and the temple in A.D. 70 was to be a sign to the Jews, and the world, that God had wrought a mighty transformation from one covenant to another. The disciples knew this was a predicted work of God, for these are the words of Jesus, the Son of God. These events that Jesus prophesied would be a sign that He was the Messiah and that He was ruling from the heavens. This would be the sign that the Son of man was in heaven.

> *And then shall appear the sign of the Son of man in heaven and then shall all the tribes of the earth mourn, and they shall see the Son of man coming in the clouds of heaven with power and great glory.* (Matt. 24:30)

Several translations of the scripture placed the word *appear* after the words *of the Son of Man*, conveying that a sign would appear in heaven or the sky. Reading these words would make us think that the *sign* was Jesus appearing in the sky in reference to the final coming. The King James Version and other translations place the word *appear* more appropriately before the word *sign*. This communicates that when the *sign appears*, this reveals the Son of man is in heaven.

Notice, the *New King James Version* says: "Then the sign of the Son of Man will **appear in heaven**, and then all the tribes of the earth will mourn" (Matt. 24:30). (Emphasis mine.)

This translation leads many to believe that it is referring to the Son of Man as appearing in the sky or heaven. Now, notice the *King James Version* places the word *appear* before the word *sign*: "And then shall **appear the sign** of the Son of man in heaven: and then shall all the tribes of the earth mourn" (Matt. 24:30).

The Greek-English Interlinear study helps display the Greek text as it would read in the literal translation of the original, thus giving us an authoritative means of examining the verse. "And then will **appear the sign** of the Son of Man in heaven, and then will bewail all the tribes of the land and they will see the Son of Man coming on the clouds of heaven with power and glory much" (Matt. 24:30). [The Greek-English Interlinear] (Emphasis mine.)

The actual Greek-English translation reveals more accurately that it is the sign that shall appear, indicating that the Son of Man is in heaven. We can have confidence in this form of interpretation because of the "law of context." Keeping this prophecy in its contextual authority reveals Jesus is not speaking of His second coming at the end of history, but rather, He is tying His prophecy of the temple destruction to the evidence that the Son of Man is in heaven.

Coming on the Clouds

Jesus told his disciples they would see His coming on the clouds of heaven with power and great glory. He used similar words when He told His disciples that some of them would not die until they saw the Son of Man coming in his Kingdom.

For the Son of man shall come in the glory of his Father with his angels; and then he shall reward every man according to his works. Verily I say unto you, There be some standing here, which shall not taste of death, till they see the Son of man coming in his kingdom. (Matt. 16:27, 28)

Adam Clarke's Commentary explains Matthew 16:27:

For the Son of man shall come in the glory of his Father—This seems to refer to Daniel 7:13, Daniel 7:14. "Behold, one like the Son of man came to the ancient of Days and there was given him dominion, and glory, and a kingdom, that all people, and nations, and languages should serve him." This was the glorious Mediatorial kingdom which Jesus Christ was now about to set up, by the destruction of the Jewish nation and polity, and the diffusion of his Gospel through the whole world. If the words be taken in this sense, the angels or messengers may signify the apostles and their successors in the sacred ministry, preaching the Gospel in the power of the Holy Ghost. It is very likely that the words do not apply to the final judgment, to which they are generally referred; but to the wonderful display of God's grace and power after the day of Pentecost.[58]

Gary DeMar explains the importance of these verses and what it means for the Son of Man to come in power and great glory.

Matthew 24:30 states that Jesus' disciples will "see" His coming. Earlier in the gospel Jesus tells His disciples that some of them would live long enough to "see the Son of Man coming in His kingdom" (16:28). Jesus told His accusers in Matthew 26:64, "Hereafter you shall see the Son of Man sitting at the right hand of power, and coming on the clouds of heaven." Those people to

---

[58] *Adam Clarke's Commentary*

whom Jesus spoke did "see the Son of Man." The event had to take place before all of them died. Before that generation passed away they must have seen the "Son of Man coming in His kingdom" and "sitting at the right hand of power." If we deny that this happened, then we are asserting that the Bible is in error.[59]

The words used by Jesus, "coming on the clouds," is a biblical expression that is not familiar with most people in our present day. At first, one might think this is a reference to the second coming of Christ. The angel did say that this same Jesus would come in like manner as you see Him go away as the clouds hid Him out of their sight (Acts 1:11). Jesus' ascension included the clouds hiding Him, while "coming on the clouds," is a biblical term referring to the power and authority of Christ being revealed before the Jewish tribes of Israel. The tribes of the *earth* which is translated as *land,* which are the Jewish tribes of Israel, will *see the Son of Man coming on the clouds.* As mentioned above, we have a conflict with modern day English and biblical language. The words *coming on the clouds* are often used in the Bible to speak of judgment of a local situation or the manifestation of God's power.

One such reference is God's deliverance of David from Saul as recorded in Psalms:

Then the earth shook and trembled; the foundations of the hills also quaked and were shaken, because He was angry. Smoke went up from His nostrils, and devouring fire from His mouth; coals were kindled by it. He bowed the heavens also, and came down with darkness under His feet. And He rode upon a cherub, and flew; he flew upon the wings of the wind. He made darkness His secret place; **his canopy around Him was dark waters and thick clouds of the skies**. *From the brightness*

---

[59] DeMar, 158.

*before Him, **his thick clouds** passed with hailstones and coals of fire. The LORD also thundered from heaven, and the Most High uttered His voice, hailstones and coals of fire. He sent out His arrows and scattered the foe, lightning in abundance, and He vanquished them.* (Ps. 18:7-14) (Emphasis mine)

It seems that David gets carried away with language of hyperbole. He speaks of the earth shaking, the foundations of mountains moving, fire coming out of God's mouth, smoke coming from His nostrils, God coming on dark clouds, riding upon the winds, sending hailstones and coals of fire, sending arrows, and making the foundations of the world uncovered. All of this is used just to declare that God gave David victory from his enemies. A reader who does not understand biblical language might think that David is speaking of the end of the world and God coming in His last day judgment, but in fact, he is simply describing a victory for himself over Saul who sought his life. If such language is used to characterize one small victory for one man, why would it be out of proportion for Jesus to use the same language to depict His coming in judgment against apostate Israel those who had rejected His Messiahship?

Stanley Paher, in his book entitled *If Thou Hadst Known*, explains how clouds are used to speak of God's presence and His coming in judgment:

Jeremiah declared that God shall come up as clouds on Judah (4:13). These were clouds of destruction. Similarly, Jesus would not literally be present in Jerusalem in 70 A.D., but would come in judgment with the use of the Roman armies. His "presence" would be so real that all would recognize His influence in the destruction of the City, just as though they had seen Him with their own eyes.

Several other Old Testament passages associate God with clouds. In Exodus 13:22 Jehovah went before the people by day in a pillar of a cloud. He descended in a cloud at Mt. Sinai at the deliverance of the law (Ex. 34:5). He appeared in a cloud upon the mercy seat after Aaron's sons died (Lev. 16:2). In the temple the glory of Jehovah was in a cloud (I Kings 8:10-11); clouds are round about Him (Psa. 97:2). In Psalm 104:3 God makes the clouds his chariot, Psalm 18:10-12: "At the brightness before him His thick clouds passed." In Ezekiel's description of a vision of Jehovah (1:4), a great cloud contained God's four living creatures.[60]

Jesus told the High Priest, who asked Him if He was the Christ, He said, "It is as you said. Nevertheless, I say to you, hereafter you will see the Son of Man sitting at the right hand of the Power, and coming on the clouds of heaven" (Matt. 26:64). *Coming on the clouds of heaven* meant that Jesus would be given full dominion at the Father's right hand in heaven.

In the synoptic Gospel of Luke, concerning this same account, this connection is made for us by Jesus Himself. "Hereafter the Son of Man will sit on the right hand of the power of God" (Luke 22:69). Jesus tells us that *coming on the clouds* means the same thing as "sitting on the right hand of power." In Luke, the words, "coming on the clouds," were not used; however, Jesus was speaking of the same subject and answering the same question. Luke leaves out, *coming on the clouds,* because it meant the same as having all power.

"Coming with the clouds" are the words that Daniel used to speak of Jesus' ascension to power and glory. Dispensationalists use Daniel 7:14 to point to a future day when Christ will be crowned

---

[60] Stanley W. Paher, *If Thou Hadst Known* (Las Vegas, Nevada, Neva Publications, 1978), 98, 99.

King of Kings; however, Daniel speaks of Jesus' ascension and His rule from heaven:

> *I was watching in the night visions, and behold, One like the Son of Man, coming with the clouds of heaven! He came to the Ancient of Days, and they brought Him near before Him. Then to Him was given dominion and glory and a kingdom, that all peoples, nations, and languages should serve Him. His dominion is an everlasting dominion, which shall not pass away, and His kingdom the one which shall not be destroyed.* (Dan. 7:13, 14)

The prophet Daniel saw the ascension of Jesus as He came before the Ancient of Days (Father God). One like the Son of Man was given dominion, glory, and a kingdom that would never be destroyed. Notice, this coming was the Son of Man *coming up* before the Ancient of Days. He was *not descending* in this coming, but rather *ascending*. This coming in power and on the clouds, spoke of Christ's ascension and Christ being given a kingdom and dominion.

Gathering of the Elect

> *And He will send His angels with a great sound of a trumpet, and they will gather together His elect from the four winds, from one end of heaven to the other.* (Matt. 24:31)

With Jesus crowned King of kings and sitting upon the throne in heaven, He sends out His messengers to the whole world to gather (synagogue), the elect into the kingdom. With Jerusalem destroyed and the temple gone, only the kingdom of God remains. This verse depicts the preaching of the gospel and the gaining of converts from among the scattered tribes as well as from the Gentiles. "The Greek word translated 'angels' is simply the common word used for 'messengers,' God's prophets, messengers, and ministers, both in the Old and New Testament, are described as His angels."[61]

The gospel began to go out to all the world after Pentecost, beginning with the Jew first and then the Gentiles. When the temple was destroyed, the gathering of all believers was truly from all "four winds" meaning all four parts of the earth. DeMar expounds more fully:

> *Matthew 24:31 draws on Old Testament imagery: trumpet, four winds, from one end of the sky to another. The trumpet is symbolic of a great work about to commence, the great gathering of God's people into a new nation. The word for "gather" is the Greek word synagogue. A gathering of Jews met in a synagogue, Judaism, in its rejection of Christ, had become a "synagogue of Satan" (Revelation 2:9; 3:9). The true synagogue of God—the church—is made up of believing Jews and Gentiles. The elect are scattered around the world, "from the four winds, from one end of the sky to the other" (cf. Matthew 28:18-20). God heralds the great ingathering of His elect from every tribe, tongue, and nation by sending His gospel messengers into the world (John 11:51-52; Revelation 7:9).*[62]

Paul tells us the elect, or the Israel of God, made up of both Jews and Gentiles, would be gathered through salvation from the four ends of the earth. Jesus uses the words, "from the four winds." It is a reference to the entire world. DeMar explains: "The phrase 'the four corners of the earth,' is a common expression for the four points of the compass, that is, from around the world. Jesus was emphasizing the fact that under the new covenant His elect are gathered from

---

everywhere."[63] Christ declares He will send his messengers with the sound of a trumpet. *Adam Clarke' Commentary* interprets the sound of the trumpet as, "the earnest affectionate call of the Gospel of peace, life, and salvation."[64]

Jesus' most detailed prophecy was declared and fulfilled within the time of the first-generation Christians. Jesus used the fig tree with tender leaves right before summer as an example. In the same way, they would know when all these things would take place in their generation. He declares once more, *this generation will not pass away until all these things take place* (Matt. 24:34). Dispensation-alists use the analogy of a fig tree to represent modern day Israel becoming a nation. They interpret Jesus to say, when all these things begin to take place, then the generation living at that time will not pass away until all is fulfilled. They also substitute the word *race* for *generation* inferring that Jesus is saying Jews will not pass away until all is fulfilled. The Greek word for "generation" is *genea,* and is never translated as race.

Many great expositors interpreted Jesus' words in Matthew 24, Luke 21, and Mark 13, to be fulfilled completely in that generation:

John Gill (1766): "This is a full and clear proof, that not any thing that is said before [v. 34], relates to the second coming of Christ, the day of judgment, and the end of the world; but that all belongs to the coming of the son of man in the destruction of Jerusalem, and to the end of the Jewish state."[65]

John Lightfoot (1658): "Hence it appears plain enough, that the foregoing verses [Matt. 24:1–34] are not to be understood of

---

[63] Gary DeMar, *End Times Fiction, A Biblical Consideration for the Left Behind Theology* (Nashville, TN: Thomas Nelson Publisher, 2001), 108, 109.
[64] *Adam Clarke's Commentary,* Matthew 24:31
[65] John Gill, *An Exposition of the New Testament,* 3 vols. (London: Matthews and Leigh, 1809), 1:296.

the last judgment, but, as we said, of the destruction of Jerusalem. There were some among the disciples (particularly John), who lived to see these things come to pass. With Matt. xvi. 28, compare John xxi. 22. And there were some Rabbins [*sic*] alive at the time when Christ spoke these things, that lived until the city was destroyed."[66]

Thomas Newton (1755): "It is to me a wonder how any man can refer part of the foregoing discourse to the destruction of Jerusalem, and part to the end of the world, or any other distant event, when it is said so positively here in the conclusion, *All these things shall be fulfilled in this generation.*"[67]

This has great meaning for us today. The King of kings is still in charge of the nations. He rules from the heavens through the power of the gospel. He has full authority and has commissioned the church to reign with Him until He has put all enemies under His feet. When He has abolished all rule and all authority and power, He will deliver the kingdom over to the God and Father, that God may be all in all.

We have confidence that the work of Christ on the cross is sufficient to transform individuals, families, communities, and nations. The kingdom of God is, as Daniel the prophet declared, the little stone that becomes a huge mountain and fills all the earth. We need not fear of those things that come upon the earth, as our Lord sits on His throne and rules in the affairs of men and nations.

---

[66] John Lightfoot, *A Commentary on the New Testament from the Talmud and Hebraica,* 4 vol. (Oxford: Oxford University Press, [1658-1674] 1859), 2:320.

[67] Newton, Thomas, *Dissertations on the prophecies: which have remarkably been fulfilled and at this time are fulfilling in the world.* London: Longman 1832, 377.

The Sign of the Kingdom
Discussion Questions

1. What appears in heaven, the sign or the Son of Man?

2. What is the sign that the Son of man is in heaven?

3. What principle of interpretation gives us the confidence that Jesus is not predicting his second coming at the end of the world?

4. When the Bible says that God rides on the clouds (Ps 104:3), what is being said?

5. In Daniel 7:13-14, the Son of man is coming up instead of coming down. To what is this in reference?

6. What does the word *gather* mean (Matt. 24:31)?

7. What are some of the terms given to the generation in which the elect was being saved?

    1.

    2.

    3.

Conclusion

The darkest days are behind us. The light has come. There are no darker days in history than the days without Christ and without a revelation of God's word. These were the days before Christ came. The commandments of God had been made null and void by the traditions of the Jewish elders. Only a remnant of believers remained.

Isaiah prophesied these days. He declared, "Arise, shine, for your light has come, and the glory of the Lord rises upon you. See, darkness covers the earth and thick darkness is over the peoples, but the Lord rises upon you and his glory appears over you" (Isa 60:1-2).

Christ is the light and Isaiah was foretelling this more than seven hundred years before He came. Jesus, the light of the world, has come and it is not dark anymore. Paul wrote the Colossians telling us of this work of Christ, "For he has rescued us from the dominion of darkness and brought us into the kingdom of the Son he loves" (Col 1:13). Peter reminds us that we have been called out of darkness into His wonderful light. It is not dark any more. The Light has come.

Christ sits on His throne and is presently reigning, and must reign until every enemy is placed under his feet. The last enemy to be destroyed is death. That means He is reigning now, from the time of His ascension until the resurrection, then He turns the kingdom over to His Father (1 Cor 15). If His enemies are put under His feet, then that references His body. The Church is His body and we obviously participate with Christ in His present reign seeing the gospel go forth into all the nations. The power of the cross changes individuals, families, communities, and nations. Jesus told us to go and make disciple of all nations.

Christ reigns through the gospel. Those who believe will be saved and those who do not, will be damned. That may sound strong, but it reminds us of what John says in the Book of Revelation, that He rules with an iron scepter. He dashes them to pieces like pottery (Rev 2:27).

This gospel must go forth to all the nations because the nations belong to Him. God told the Son to ask for the nations as His inheritance. The nations that refuse to kiss the Son will perish from the earth (Psalm 2), meaning the meek will inherit the earth. The meek are those who humble themselves and believe in Christ.

This kingdom which began as a small stone is becoming a huge mountain that fills all the earth. It is as Jesus declared, that the kingdom is like leaven that increases until the whole lump is filled. That is what is presently happening now. The gospel through the Church extends the kingdom, and it continues to increase throughout history. The Church is the most victorious entity in the earth. Christ wins, the Church wins, and the kingdom and His government increases with no end.

David Chilton reminds us of one of the powerful quotes from Charles H. Spurgeon, by placing it on the cover of his book, *Paradise Restored*:

> *I myself believe that King Jesus will reign, and the idols be utterly abolished; but I expect the same power which turned the*

world upside down once will still continue to do it. The Holy Ghost would never suffer the imputation to rest upon His holy name that He was unable to convert the world.[68]

The prophet Isaiah declared, "the mountain of the Lord's temple will be established as the highest of the mountains; it will be exalted above the hills, and all nations will stream to it" (Isa 2:2). He later declares that when the light comes, which is Christ, "The nations will come to your light, and kings to the brightness of your dawn" (Isa 60:3). The same prophet announced, "for the earth will be filled with the knowledge of the Lord as the waters cover the sea" (Isa 11:9).

We are the children of Abraham through Christ, and the Church is the fulfillment of all that God had in mind. Christ and the Gospel will continue until the nations belong to the Lord and then He will return in power and great glory. This is a victorious Christology which means our eschatology is victorious.

---

[68] David Chilton, *Paradise Restored, A Biblical Theology of Dominion* (Ft Worth, TX: Dominion Press, 1985), back cover.

Bibliography

Adam Clarke's Commentary. Matthew 24:29.

Adam Clarke's Commentary. Vol 1, Matthew-Acts

Boettner, Loraine. *The Millennium.* Phillipsburg, NJ: Presbyterian and Reformed Publishing, 1957

Bray, John L. *Israel in Bible Prophecy.* Lakeland, FL: John L. Bray Ministries, Inc, 1983

Bray, John L. *Matthew 24 Fulfilled.* Lakeland, FL: John L Bray Ministries Inc, 1996

Calvin, John. *Calvin's Commentaries,* vol. XXI. Trans. William Pringle. Grand Rapids, MI: Baker Book House, reprint ed. 1979

Chilton, David. *Paradise Restored, A Biblical Theology of Dominion.* Ft, Worth, TX: Dominion Press, 1985

Crenshaw, Curtis I. and Grover E. Gunn, III. *Dispensationalism Today, Yesterday, and Tomorrow.* Memphis, TN: Footstool Publishing, 1985

DeMar, Gary. *End Times Fiction, A Biblical Consideration for the Left Behind Theology.* Nashville, TN: Thomas Nelson Publisher, 2001

DeMar, Gary. *Is Jesus Coming Soon?* Power Spring, GA: American Vision Inc., 2006. First edition, 1999

DeMar, Gary. *Last Days Madness, Obsession of the Modern Church.* Atlanta, GA: American Vision, 1994

Eusebius. *The Nicene and Post-Nicene Fathers.* Grand Rapids, MI: Wm. B. Eerdmans, Reprint, 1979

Gill, John. *An Exposition of the New Testament,* 3 vols. London: Matthews and Leigh, 1809

Hagee, John. *Beginning of the End, The Assassination of Yitzhak Rabin and the Coming Antichrist.* Nashville, TN: Thomas Nelson Publishers, 1996

John Gill's Exposition of the Bible, Matthew 24:27

Josephus, *Jewish War,* bk. v. c. x.

Josephus, *Jewish Wars* c. xiii.

Josephus, *Antiquities,* XVIII.IX.8, 395.

Kik, Marcellus J. *An Eschatology of Victory,* Phillipsburg, NJ: Presbyterian and Reformed, 1971

LaHaye, Tim. *The Beginning of the End.* Wheaton, Il: Tyndale House Publishers, 1982

Lande, William L. *Commentary on the Gospel of Mark.* Grand Rapids, MI: Eerdmans, 1974

Larkin, Clarence. *The Greatest Book on Dispensational Truth in the World*. Philadelphia, PA: Rev. Clarence Larkin Est., 1920

Lightfoot, John. *A Commentary on the New Testament from the Talmud and Hebraica*. 4 vol. Oxford: Oxford University Press, 1859

Lindsey, Hal. *The Late Great Planet Earth*. Grand Rapids, MI: Zondervan Publishing House, 1980

Newton, Thomas. *Dissertations on the prophecies: which have remarkably been fulfilled and at this time are fulfilling in the world*. London: Longman 1832

Newton, Thomas. *Dissertations on the Prophecies*, 389; also see Eusebius, *Ecclesiastical History*, Bk 3, chapter 5; Edersheim, *Life and Times of Jesus the Messiah*, 448.

Paher, Stanley W. *If Thou Hadst Known*. Las Vegas, NV: Neva Publications, 1978

Pelikan, Jaroslav, editor. English translation from *Lectures on Galatians*, 1519, in volume 27 of *Luther's Works*. Saint Louis, MO: Concordia, 1964

Roberts, Alexander and James Donaldson, eds. Circa AD 160. English translation from the *Dialogue* with Trypho xi, in *The Ante-Nicene Fathers of the Christian Church*, vol. 1. Grand Rapids, MI: Eerdmans. Repr., 1987

Spurgeon, Charles H. *The Treasury of David*. Psalm 89.

Tacitus. *The Histories*. Trans. Clifford H. Moore. Cambridge, MA: Harvard University, 1962

The Works of Flavius Josephus. Vol.1,3 *The Wars of the Jews*, 4:9:2.

Vassiliades, "New Testament Ecclesiological Perspectives on Laity", p.348. Acts 9:31,41; 26:19; Gal. 6:16; Rom. 1:7; 8:27, 33; 12:13; 15:25; Col. 3:12; 1 Peter 2:9.

Woodrow, Ralph. *Great Prophecies of the Bible.* Riverside, CA: Ralph Woodrow Evangelistic Association, 1971

www.ingramcontent.com/pod-product-compliance
Lightning Source LLC
LaVergne TN
LVHW021510080426
835509LV00018B/2463